BUILDING A COMMUNITY-CONTROLLED ECONOMY:
THE EVANGELINE CO-OPERATIVE EXPERIENCE

This case study focuses on and analyses the development of four co-operatives in the Evangeline region, a small Acadian community in the south-west part of Prince Edward Island.

Defined by the authors as an 'integrated community-controlled economy,' the Evangeline community demonstrates the potential that a network of interrelated co-operatives has for community economic development. More specifically, the authors discuss why some co-operatives succeed while others fail and propose a model that outlines the elements necessary for any comprehensive community economic development process.

Wilkinson and Quarter look at the Evangeline experiment in the context of two seemingly contradictory trends today: globalization and decentralization. They argue that the initiatives undertaken by the Evangeline community fit within the trend toward decentralization and community control. The citizens of the Evangeline region have organized a community-controlled economy, refusing to accept the conventional wisdom that a small community is not viable in a modern economy. The authors suggest that the Evangeline experiment shows that communities that are being marginalized in the modern world can take matters into their own hands and succeed where externally driven development has failed.

PAUL WILKINSON is a Community Development Consultant with the Saskatchewan Department of Social Services.

JACK QUARTER is a professor at the Ontario Institute for Studies in Education of the University of Toronto, and author of *Canada's Social Economy* and *Crossing the Line*. He is co-editor of *How to Start a Worker Co-op* and *Partners in Enterprise: The Worker Ownership Phenomenon*.

T0338883

PAUL WILKINSON AND JACK QUARTER

Building a Community-Controlled Economy: The Evangeline Co-operative Experience

UNIVERSITY OF TORONTO PRESS
Toronto Buffalo London

© University of Toronto Press Incorporated 1996
Toronto Buffalo London
Printed in Canada

ISBN 0-8020-0873-9 (cloth)
ISBN 0-8020-7857-5 (paper)

Printed on acid-free paper

Canadian Cataloguing in Publication Data

Wilkinson, Paul
    Building a community-controlled economy : the Evangeline
    co-operative experience

    Includes bibliographical references.
    ISBN 0-8020-0873-9 (bound)   ISBN 0-8020-7857-5 (pbk.)

    1. Cooperation – Prince Edward Island – Évangéline Region.
    2. Cooperative societies – Prince Edward Island –
    Évangéline Region.   3. Évangéline Region (P.E.I.) –
    Economic policy.   I. Quarter, Jack, 1941– .   II. Title.
    HD3450.A3P75 1996   334'.09717'1   C96-931108-7

University of Toronto Press acknowledges the financial assistance to its
publishing program of the Canada Council and the Ontario Arts Council.

This book has been published with the help of a grant from the Humanities
and Social Sciences Federation of Canada, using funds provided by the Social
Sciences and Humanities Research Council of Canada.

To the members of Evangeline co-operatives and to volunteers everywhere, who contribute in some small way to improving the quality of their communities.

Contents

Preface

The bold experiment in building a community-controlled economy undertaken in Evangeline, Prince Edward Island, can be seen in the context of two seemingly contradictory trends in the world today. One of these trends, represented by globalization, is reducing the ability of nation states to carry out policies desired by their citizenry. Increasingly the political and economic decision-making power of states is being transferred to multinational corporations and supranational organizations, accountable only to themselves. At the same time, there is a counter-trend toward the decentralization of decision-making power to regions and communities. This trend is fuelled by the desire of citizens to retain some control over the institutions that govern them. It reflects a rejection of top-down solutions and is indicative of a positive desire to participate in decisions affecting local communities.

The initiatives described in this manuscript fit within the trend to decentralization and community control. Citizens of the Evangeline region of Prince Edward Island have refused to accept the conventional wisdom that their tiny community is not viable in a modern economy. Instead they have intentionally set about creating a community-controlled economy through an interrelated network of co-operative organizations. By so doing, they offer hope to communities routinely passed over by conventional economic approaches to development. Indeed the Evangline experience suggests that communities that are being marginalized in the modern world – for example, rural, inner city, and aboriginal – can take matters into their own hands and succeed where externally driven development efforts have failed.

In addition, the Evangeline experience suggests that it is possible to create an economy in which economic organizations exist to promote the general community welfare rather than simply to benefit individual interest. Through the analysis of Evangeline that follows, we hope that theoreticians and practitioners will draw insights that will assist in their understanding both the key components of a community-controlled economy and the strategies that are most likely to succeed in developing such an economy. In other words, it is our hope that this manuscript may contribute in some small way to the building of a democratically accountable economy.

We would like to thank Virgil Duff, executive editor at University of Toronto Press; Darlene Money, our copy-editor; Madhumita Pal, our indexer; and Alison Davidson, who assisted with the proofreading, for helping to bring this book to completion. Appreciation is also extended to Angela Miles, Jack Craig, Budd Hall, and Harold Baker for comments upon an earlier version. We wish also to express our appreciation to the members of the Evangeline co-operatives who agreed to be interviewed. Their names appear in the book. Of these, Amand Arsenault and Claudette McNeill must be singled out for special recognition. They graciously took time away from their work and volunteer activities to provide background information and advice. They also went out of their way to make the field researcher feel welcome in the community, with invitations to clam diggings, house parties, and lobster fishing. Thanks are also due to Evangeline and Freddy Gallant for the wonderful way that they opened their home to the field researcher during the period that the interviews were being conducted.

PAUL WILKINSON AND JACK QUARTER

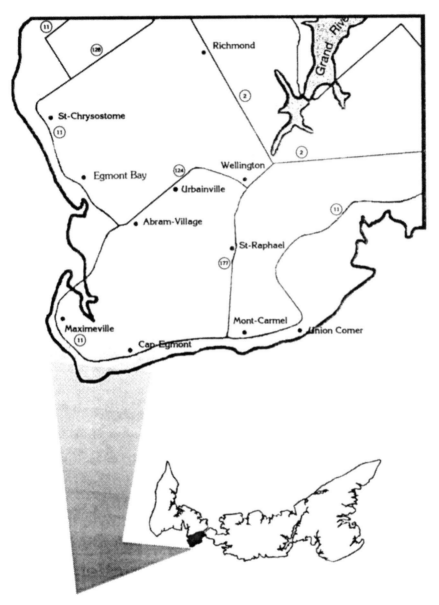

THE EVANGELINE REGION. This map first appeared in *Profile de la Région Évangéline*. It is reproduced by permission of Amand Arsenault, Evangeline Regional Services Centre.

BUILDING A COMMUNITY-CONTROLLED ECONOMY:

THE EVANGELINE CO-OPERATIVE EXPERIENCE

1

The Evangeline Co-operative Tradition

In April 1990, fifty-one years after the incorporation of their first co-operative store, eight hundred people from the Evangeline region of Prince Edward Island turned out in minus twenty degree weather to celebrate the opening of their new supermarket. The speaker for the occasion, Reverend Eloi Arsenault, stressed the significant role that co-operatives have played in the life of Evangeline people: 'Co-operatives have been the key to the social and economic development of the community' (Van Vliet 1990, 23). Indeed this twenty-square-kilometre area, with only twenty-five hundred residents, has been called 'the uncontested co-operative capital of North America' (R. Arsenault 1988, 7). Its sixteen co-operatives are a social infrastructure for the community, providing its most basic services from the cradle to the grave.

The co-operatives have a combined membership of 5,811, or 2.5 per resident of the community (including children), and are extremely diversified in function, offering a wide range of services, creating employment, and providing leadership in community and cultural development. Not only do the co-operatives play a significant part in people's daily lives, but they are viewed as vehicles for community development. Their mandate is to respond to the needs of the entire Evangeline region rather than simply to function for the benefit of the members of a particular organization.

Consequently the Evangeline co-operatives have acted somewhat differently from those in other areas. Whereas co-operatives often emphasize economic objectives, in the Evangeline region a number of co-operatives have been set up specifically for cultural reasons. The arts co-operative, for example, exists to teach and promote Acadian culture; the cable co-operative has the dual mandate of providing a service on an economic basis and of encouraging retention of the French language. Another difference is the widespread support that the region's co-operatives have shown for the establishment of worker co-operatives. When community members wanted to start worker co-operatives to manufacture potato chips and children's clothing, the Evangeline Co-operative Council organized a special training program and the Evangeline Credit Union put in place the Baie Acadienne Venture Capital Group to provide the new co-operatives with equity financing.

Most interesting of all has been the creation of the Co-operative Council (Conseil Coopératif) with representatives from all co-operatives in the region. This council, a second-tier co-operative, pulls together the primary co-operatives (in which individuals are members) to consider regional needs, conduct educational activities, and assist in the development of new co-operatives. In short, it plays a leadership role in the cultural and economic development of the region.

In terms of the region's economy, the contribution of the co-operatives is a significant one, providing more employment than both government and private sector combined. In 1990, a total of 352 persons from the region (total population of 2500) were employed, either full-time or seasonally full-time, by co-operatives, and another 14 persons were employed on a part-time basis. To put these figures into perspective, one person from every two households in Evangeline is employed in a co-operative. The payroll for these employees amounted to $1.99 million, and, in addition, the value of goods purchased in the area by co-operatives was $30.5 million (C. Gallant 1991).

Therefore, co-operatives have played a somewhat different role in community development in Evangeline than in other regions of Canada. Although there are other communities in Canada (for example, Chéticamp, Nova Scotia) and throughout the Western world (Mondragon in Basque Spain, Emilia Romagna in northern Italy, the kibbutzim of Israel) in which there are integrated systems of co-operatives pursuing a broad set of social objectives around the development of a community, these are the exceptions rather than the rule. Generally co-operatives have been oriented toward serving a membership, and their external relations are to other co-operatives providing a similar service – for example, credit unions belonging to a central organization of other credit unions. This functional form of outreach is designed to strengthen the ability of the primary organization to provide its service rather than to serve the broader objective of developing the local community. These functional arrangements might also strengthen the local community, but unlike Evangeline the co-operation between co-operatives is not normally part of a systematic exercise in planning for the future development of the community. Therefore, the most striking feature of the Evangeline model is the way that the various co-operatives are linked together to pursue a community development strategy for the entire region.

THE COMMUNITY FABRIC

Evangeline is situated on the south-west coast of Prince Edward Island, a tiny province of only 2100 square miles in the Gulf of St Lawrence, a short ferry ride from New Brunswick. The Evangeline community, made up of the parish of Mont-Carmel and the municipalities of Wellington and Abram-Village (both small villages), is about 15 miles from Summerside and about an hour's drive from Charlottetown, the provincial capital. At one time farming and forestry contributed significantly to the region's economy, but their importance has declined. Fishing, on the other hand, has retained its importance as the economic mainstay of the region, providing jobs for some 100 fishers and their helpers, while another 150 community members work in the co-operative lobster-canning plant.

   In recent years the decentralization of provincial government services to the regional level has brought a certain number of civil service jobs to the community. Also a degree of economic diversification has been achieved in the past twenty-five years through the establishment of both private and co-operative enterprises for tourism services, agricultural processing, and the manufacture of natural fertilizer from seaweed and lobster shells. Small-scale construction and boat building also provide a significant level of employment.

One distinctive feature of Evangeline is the tightly knit social relationships based upon the Acadian culture, the French language, the Roman Catholic religion, and, even more so, extended family ties as reflected in such common surnames as Arsenault, Gallant, and Bernard. The close interpersonal relationships, a factor that has been assisted by the concentration of Acadians in the region, has been important in the retention of their culture and language in the face of surrounding anglophone domination. In the Evangeline region of P.E.I., persons of Acadian descent make up over seventy-five per cent of the population, whereas outside of Evangeline persons of Acadian ancestry are widely dispersed among the English-speaking majority, where they have had an uphill battle to maintain their language and cultural institutions. As a result assimilation has taken its toll, with the consequent loss of the French language. Georges Arsenault, the author of a recent history of Prince Edward Island's Acadians, reports that 'over fifty per cent of Island Acadians can only speak English. Numerous Acadian communities are almost entirely English-speaking' (1989, 255).

In the Evangeline region, by comparison, seventy-five per cent of the people still speak French at home, and the Acadian traditions are practised widely. The residents of Evangeline fought for and achieved the right to choose their own school board and to educate their children in French. This success provided the springboard for other cultural initiatives, such as the establishment of a co-operative medical centre to provide bilingual services, the organization of a cable co-operative to bring in French-language television, and the organization of an arts co-operative to encourage creative cultural expression. One of the most interesting cultural initiatives is the Acadian Festival, which is held each year during the last week of August. At this annual celebration, cultural identity is strengthened and reaffirmed as local talent performs traditional Acadian music and dance before thousands of appreciative visitors, both from the Acadian diaspora and other tourists that are passing through.

Thus there are three distinct features of development in Evangeline: it is locally owned and controlled; it harmonizes social and economic goals in ways that are compatible with community's culture and values; and the primary structure is an interrelated system of co-operative corporations, or what might be labelled as collective entrepreneurship. The combination of these factors makes Evangeline an interesting laboratory. The residents have collectively taken charge of their own development according to their customs and traditions through the mechanism of co-operatives. Unlike other regions where the centralization of large co-operative corporations has led to their losing touch with the local community, in Evangeline community control and accountability have been retained. In addition, Evangeline has developed innovative mechanisms such as the Co-operative Council to encourage and guide development for the benefit of the entire community.

Moreover, Evangeline is situated in a part of Canada that has been below the national average with respect to income and generally has suffered an out-migration of people due to high unemployment and below-average participation rates in the economy. The fact that a community in a region of the country targeted for regional development programs has initiated an innovative approach is an additional reason for attempting to understand the dynamics that are producing the results.

EVANGELINE AND THE REGIONAL-DEVELOPMENT
TRADITION

The Evangeline approach to development is part of the regional development tradition in Canada – albeit a unique part of it. Since the 1930s, when the federal government started giving aid to prairie farmers, there has been a tradition in Canada to assist the development of businesses in so-called underdeveloped regions of the country. By 1969 these programs were consolidated within the federal Department of Regional Economic Expansion (DREE), and then in 1984 they were decentralized, with the Atlantic Canada Opportunities Agency (ACOA) in Moncton controlling programs for the four Atlantic provinces, and the Western Diversification Initiative dealing with the Western provinces. Although there are many types of regional development programs, a primary government strategy for communities in circumstances similar to Evangeline has been to give incentives to outside industries to relocate there. Such initiatives may be seen as part of the philosophy of development conceived of in the West after the Second World War, which involved an effort to improve the standard of living of people in poorer regions of the world by transferring the technologies and values of the United States and other Western countries through subsidiary corporations and government-sponsored development agencies.

The limitations of this transfer or extension approach may be seen in an independent evaluation of Enterprise Cape Breton, a sub-program of the federal Atlantic Canada Opportunities Agency, until its absorption in 1991. ECB's primary strategy appeared to be to entice large corporations to establish subsidiaries in Cape Breton. It ran advertisements in the *New York Times* promising 'free money, less tax and no red tape.' The strategy proved a dismal failure, as summarized in a report of an independent assessment team hired by the federal government: 'The generous up-front and topping-up financing built into the programs reduced the equity required from the client to an extremely low level and attracted a disproportionate number of high-risk companies. Some of these companies proved unwilling or unable to see their projects through difficult times ... Branch-plant operations approved by ECB have had a low rate of success' (Cape Breton Assessment Team 1991, 112). In reflecting upon the ECB approach, former vice-chair of the organization Theresa MacNeil admitted candidly: 'It would not engage citizens. It would not because the proclaimed measures of success were dollars committed and jobs created. These were the values being fostered; not the values of shifting the dispositions and capabilities of a population to take charge of its own economy! The rush for tax credits absorbed the time of all available staff. There was neither the will to involve the population in a process of transforming their economy nor, I now realize, was there a conviction on the part of government, of senior bureaucrats, of the public itself, that there was any need to do so' (1991, 8). In line with MacNeil's viewpoint, the assessors of ECB emphasized that locally owned enterprises had a much higher success rate than those owned by outsiders.

The importance of local control in development is a view also put forward in a report of the Economic Council of Canada in 1990, which promoted community economic development as a new, decentralized approach to improving the local economy. 'Local community economic development means improvement of job opportunities, income levels and other features of the economy' (Economic Council of Canada, 3), or, in other words, the establishment of businesses that have some commitment to the local community. While this understanding of development is an improvement over previous formulations, the economic emphasis continues to devalue the importance of the social and cultural components.

Other theorists are critical of an approach to community economic development that focuses strictly upon the economic. Perry, for example, insists that community economic development flows out of a moral purpose, and it is a 'technique for redressing inequities and exploitation' (1987, 73). In a similar vein, MacLeod refers to community economic development as 'a philosophy of development which entails solidarity, local responsibility and creativity' (1989, 191). For him community economic development is an attempt to subordinate economic activity to the social and cultural needs of human beings. 'Community economic development is not neutral, it is a value-laden, conscious strategy to promote the general community welfare' (178). According to Robyn Murray, a special adviser to the Ontario government on community economic development, a primary objective should be 'political empowerment' (personal communication, 13 Feb. 1992). For the theorists who emphasize the social aspect of community economic development, a fundamental purpose is to decentralize responsibility and to empower people through both ownership and control of economic structures and through assisting them to develop critical analyses. For Blakely (1992), this means 'to create more participants and less victims.' From this perspective – and a perspective that is closely aligned with that of the Evangeline region – community economic development is viewed as building interdependencies and shared commitments among people that take into account social and cultural needs as well as those that are economic (MacLeod 1989; Sachs 1991; Swack 1992).

These approaches to community economic development may be seen as part of a new economics that starts from the premise that 'the social character of human existence is primary' (Daly and Cobb 1990, 161). They argue that an economics based on this new paradigm results in a very different understanding of development, in which the economy exists to promote community. Daly and Cobb advocate that a 'model of person-in-community calls not only for provision of goods and services to the individual, but also for an economic order that supports the pattern of relationships that make up the community' (164). Community, in this sense, represents far more than a location. 'It suggests that people are bound up with one another, sharing, despite differences, a common identity' (170). From this development perspective, compatibility with the community and its culture becomes the essential starting-point for new initiatives.

This gap between the understanding of community economic development, as represented by the Economic Council of Canada on the one hand and the proponents of the new economics on the other, points to a fundamental tension in the community economic development approach. While there is general agreement on the *strategies* of community economic development (the activation of local resources, the development of local institutions and local leadership), there are differences related to such issues as the relative priority of the social and cultural in relation to economic goals as well as the relative balance between the needs of individuals and those of the community. The lack of specified values and principles to guide the community economic development enterprise contributes to the ambiguity of the concept.

Therefore, for the purpose of this study, community economic development involves the following characteristics: First, there is local ownership and control either by a geographically defined community or by a community of common interest. Second, the emphasis goes beyond the needs of particular individuals to the need to improve the community. Third, community economic development transforms economic development by undertaking it in a manner that is compatible with community culture and values. Fourth, community economic development involves the creation of local institutions and the initiation of a long-term self-reliant process that aims to make communities more environmentally and financially sound. These characteristics of community economic development are similar to those outlined by the New Economy Development Group (1993).

In addition to the four characteristics outlined above, community economic development initiatives often involve the following: development of a community vision; enhancement of individual and collective skills; development of local leadership; support to local entrepreneurs; and creation of partnerships both within and outside the community.

MODELS OF COMMUNITY ECONOMIC DEVELOPMENT

There are at least three distinct variants of community economic development in Canada. One variant grew out of the crises in the black ghettos of the United States in the late 1960s (Perry 1987). There, people from different classes recognized that they had to take the initiative to work together to find solutions to the problems of their communities. Perry expressed the excitement of this discovery as follows: 'Suddenly it became clear that ... a neighborhood would have to consciously take its destiny in its own hands and build ... the institutions and social tools that make a community work' (9). In addition to recognizing the importance of local initiative, the inseparability of social and economic development was also recognized. As Broadhead et al. argues: 'In order for blacks (and other disadvantaged people) to achieve equality, political participation would not be enough: it would also be necessary to create new economic bases in troubled communities' (1990, 3).

A second variant of community economic development can be found in initiatives sponsored by Canadian governments from the early 1960s when, for example, the province of Manitoba organized the first community development program in Canada. Based on the notion of community organization for self-help, this program operated primarily in Indian communities not designated as reserves. Encouraged by the results, other provincial governments followed suit, while the federal government developed parallel programs for Indian reserves.

In addition to programs designed specifically for Indian and native people, the 1960s saw the federal government take initiatives to involve young people as community organizers and social animators in rural and urban communities across the country. Of these initiatives, the Company of Young Canadians and the Local Initiatives Program were the most effective in assisting communities to demand their rights and a fair share of resources. Ironically, when this occurred governments found themselves in the awkward position of having to respond to citizen demands stimulated by their own workers. As a result, political support for government-sponsored community development programs evaporated and by the mid-1970s all of these programs were gone.

Finally, the oldest tradition of community economic development is based upon the co-operative movement, through which producers and consumers have achieved a voice in the decisions that affect both their interests and those of their communities. Co-operatives are guided by a set of principles developed by the International Co-operative Alliance, the representative body for co-operatives throughout the world. The most current set of principles, adopted by the ICA in Manchester, England, in September 1995, represents a variation of the original set prepared by the Rochdale Pioneers, the founders of the first modern co-operative society in 1844, and updated subsequently by the ICA. The most current principles adopted by the ICA are: 1. voluntary and open membership; 2. democratic member control (that is, one member, one vote); 3. member economic participation (members are responsible for financing their co-operative and are also the primary beneficiaries); 4. autonomy and independence (co-operatives are autonomous self-help organizations and must not jeopardize their independence through agreements with government or external lenders); 5. education, training, and information (co-operatives have an obligation to educate their members and employees about their organization, and to inform the general public about the benefits of co-operation); 6. co-operation among co-operatives (the obligation of co-operatives to work together both to serve their members and to strengthen the co-operative movement); and 7. concern for community (the obligation of co-operatives to work for sustainable development of their communities).

According to Craig (1993), co-operatives and the broader social philosophy of co-operation are derived from the values of equality, equity, and mutual self-help. From the value of equality (all people are worthy of respect) come the principles of voluntary and open membership and democratic control. The value of equity (the idea of fairness and justice) leads to the principle of member economic participation and of concern for community. From the value of mutual self-help (collective action), a term that is often used in reference to co-operatives, come the principles of autonomy and independence, education, training and information, and co-operation among co-operatives.

Although the link between co-operatives and their community has always been implicit in co-operative development, the decision of the ICA to make this connection explicit and elevate it to a principle also reflects an attempt to make co-operatives more central to the community economic development movement and to encourage that consciousness among large established co-operatives whose connections to local communities have become more tenuous. Historically, co-operatives have played a highly visible role in the development of communities across Canada. In the

Maritimes and in Western Canada, regions whose history has been shaped by economic imperialism, powerful farm-marketing and consumer co-operatives sprang up in the twenties and thirties. In Quebec, the *caisses populaires* (financial co-operatives) appeared as a means for French-speaking people to obtain the credit that was not available from the anglophone banks. The Maritime-based Antigonish Movement in particular emphasized the importance of co-operatives as 'a tool for counteracting the power of economic interests outside each community ... as a means of self-determination' (Perry 1987, 73). Initiated by Fathers Jimmy Tompkins and Moses Coady, the Antigonish Movement promoted co-operatives as a way to reform society without revolution. In 1930, the priests were instrumental in having St Francis Xavier University establish an Extension Department that sponsored 'a general adult education program oriented toward economic and especially co-operative action' (MacPherson 1979, 131). The focal point of the program at the community level was the organization of study clubs – not just talk shops but rather mechanisms for initiating collective action. After a preliminary study of community concerns 'a single common problem would be isolated for study and joint action' (131). Great emphasis was placed on the development of local leadership through lectures, workshops, and week-long schools. The objective was to identify the sources of a community's economic problems and to organize for change through group discussion, including 'kitchen-table meetings' held in people's households. George Melnyk (1985, 20) describes this process as mobilizing 'large segments of the population to launch economic organizations for community improvement.' The Antigonish Movement played a significant role in the formation of co-operative stores, fishing co-operatives, and regional organizations like the United Maritime Fishermen. Most important of all, according to MacPherson, was the Movement's assistance in the organization of credit unions, which for the first time gave low-wage Maritimers access to credit. Antigonish, according to co-operative theorist Alex Laidlaw, empowered people 'to discover and develop their own capacities for creation' (1961, 108).

Evangeline follows directly from the Antigonish tradition. It is a variant of community economic development that is focused around co-operatives. Like Antigonish, Evangeline has relied upon such adult education techniques as kitchen-table meetings and study groups. Its economic objectives (for example, to create jobs), albeit very strong, are always set within a cultural and social context based upon the preservation of the Acadian way of life. Moreover, the Evangeline co-operatives themselves depart from tradition in that they function both as independent organizations designed to serve their members and as an interrelated system embedded within the community. Therefore, in the words of co-operative theorist Craig (1993), Evangeline would represent a form of 'comprehensive co-operation,' which goes beyond the particular co-operative organization and which includes a broader vision, in this case the well-being of the community and the Acadian people. An excellent example of comprehensive co-operation that has received much publicity is the Mondragon Group in the Basque region of Spain. There, co-operatives with a variety of functions are connected to one another by means of a governing superstructure, to form a community of co-operatives that not only serves its members but also assists in the development of the surrounding community (Whyte and Whyte 1988). Comprehensive co-operation may be contrasted to the more typical model – referred to by Melnyk (1985) as 'unifunctional' – which is limited to specific aspects of people's lives and does not address a broader set of community issues. Unifunctional co-operation springs from the individualism and self-interest of modern societies, and lacks a broader community perspective. Comprehensive co-operation, such as in Evangeline, is not simply a form of development within a community but rather a model through which communities may develop and strengthen themselves.

EVANGELINE'S HISTORICAL ROOTS

The Evangeline model of development is rooted in a rich common history that has helped to create a strong sense of community consciousness among the residents of the region. A central element in this history – and an element that has been internalized by the people – has been the oppression that their ancestors suffered at the hands of the British, starting in the seventeenth century. This feature of their culture, and the historical exclusion of the Acadians from the mainstream of Island society, has strengthened the solidarity within the community. One resident of the Evangeline region put it this way: 'We had to depend on ourselves because no one would help us' (P. Gallant, personal communication, 18 Feb. 1991). This has resulted in ongoing efforts to create institutions that maintain the Roman Catholic religion, French language, and Acadian culture. Since the Acadian resistance to anglophone dominance was primarily in response to oppression based on ethnicity and class, a community consciousness developed that was strongly associated with being Acadian. Gender equality, by comparison, has not received much attention.

The early Acadian pioneers were caught in colonial wars between the British and French. Wedged between New France and New England, Acadia (Maritimes, Gaspé Peninsula, north shore of Maine and the Magdalen Islands) was taken over by the British nine times between 1604 and 1910. This meant Island Acadians had to rely on their own resources and to co-exist with both English and French (Arsenault 1989). This continual transfer of ownership of Acadia ended in 1713 when the Treaty of Utrecht ceded the area to England. However, this peaceful interlude was only temporary. When war again broke out between France and England in 1744, France managed to conscript some Acadians to fight on her behalf. Consequently, after the war, the English governor decided in 1755 to ensure Acadians' loyalty by forcing them to swear an unconditional oath of allegiance to the king of England. When the independent-minded Acadians refused, 6,000 of a total of 10,000 were forcibly deported to New England (soon to become part of the United States). During this period 2,000 Acadians also escaped to the Île Saint-Jean (renamed Prince Edward Island in the Treaty of Paris in 1763).

After Louisbourg (located in what is now Cape Breton) fell in

1758, Acadians there, too, were ordered deported. Of the 4,400 Acadian inhabitants of Île Saint-Jean, 3,000 were rounded up and transported to France. The rest managed to hide in remote parts of the Island or fled to New France (now Quebec). In spite of all this, some managed to return, so that the census of 1798 identified a total of 675 Acadians.

For the Acadians of Île Saint-Jean, oppression did not end with the deportations. Their history since that time has been characterized by a struggle to survive economically, linguistically, and culturally in a hostile environment. After the Treaty of Paris, the land was divided into 67 lots or townships, which were granted to prominent Englishmen who were allowed to settle the area and pay rents to the Crown. In actual fact, most landowners found agents to collect the rent for them while they remained absentee landlords. The Acadians who already lived on the land were not taken into account. They became tenants on their own land and were forced to sign perpetual leases and pay high rents. As a result some moved to Cape Breton to obtain Crown land, whereas others moved to different lots only to be faced again with leases and demands for rent arrears when the landowner appeared. Georges Arsenault described the results of this resettlement as follows: 'The Acadian population was thus split into small groups scattered over the Island and the mainland. The move from one area to another weakened the demographic and geographic concentration of the Acadian community which was gradually surrounded by ... people of another culture and another language' (1989, 92). Only those Acadians who settled in the Evangeline region (Egmont Bay and Mont-Carmel) were able to avoid the dispersion. They had the good fortune to be able to buy their land from the Island government, which had confiscated it from the English owner who had never claimed it. This historical accident might in part explain the distinctiveness of the Evangeline community, because from its inception its residents were not split up like the other Acadians.

The land tenure problem continued until after Confederation when in 1875 the provincial government passed the Land Purchase Act, which forced owners to sell their land to the government. While the Island Acadians gradually gained ownership of their land from this time forward, the small size of the farms meant that their operations were marginal. Gradually family farms started to disappear as larger farmers bought them out. This trend was accelerated by the Development Plan of 1969, which saw the government purchase small farms, many of them Acadian. By 1980 there remained only three thousand of the fourteen thousand small farms that had existed on Prince Edward Island in 1911.

The Island Acadians' response to the experience of deportation and the injustices around land ownership was to keep to themselves. Georges Arsenault described them as 'a separate people' whose 'feelings of independence and suspicion were still strong ... at the end of the 1880s' (1989, 97). During the period 1860–90 the Island Acadians started to resist the dominant anglophone culture and to visibly identify with their own history and culture. The three national conventions of the Acadians held between 1881 and 1890 were extremely significant in creating solidarity between Acadians of the three Maritime Provinces. These conventions not only created an awareness of a common Acadian identity, but also formulated specific demands to defend French-language education. This latter was particularly critical because the policies of the provincial government, as represented by the School Act of 1877, had resulted in a shortage of francophone teachers and made English language instruction dominant.

The period 1890–1945 saw Island Acadians create new institutions to protect their identity, but at the same time brought increasing assimilation, especially in areas where Acadians made up only a small part of the population. In education, an Acadian Teachers' Association was formed in 1893, which undertook a number of initiatives to encourage the teaching of French. Among these initiatives were regional teachers' assemblies (which included parents) and summer courses in French language instruction. Other significant actions taken during this period included the launching of a French-language newspaper and annual 'national' conferences at a provincial level to increase awareness of the Acadian situation. Perhaps most important was the creation of the St Thomas Aquinas Society, an organization dedicated to cultural preservation, which has now become the main voice for the Acadian people of Prince Edward Island.

In spite of these initiatives, the erosion of the French language continued. This was to some extent due to lack of support for the French language by the Department of Education, but also the overall hegemony of anglophone culture played a part. 'Living in a milieu where the French language and culture were not highly regarded outside the home,' Arsenault argues, 'many Acadians lost interest in French education' (1989, 224).

While pressures to assimilate accelerated during the period 1945–1980, Acadians continued to struggle to maintain their culture and institutions. In 1952, the Acadian Teachers' Association prepared its own program for teaching French and distributed it to Acadian schools. In 1953 the St Thomas Aquinas Society launched a student bursary program for young Acadians taking their teacher-training courses in French. In 1960, the three parishes in the Evangeline region took advantage of new provincial legislation encouraging consolidated school boards to create their own regional high school in Abram-Village. After 1963, elementary schools as well came under the jurisdiction of the central school board, which was allowed to use French as the language for both teaching and administration. Unfortunately other Acadian schools outside the Evangeline region did not fare so well. In 1972 when all school boards were consolidated into larger administrative units, they became part of the overall anglophone-dominated school system. In these schools, French was taught only as a second language. This change also spelled the end of the Acadian Teachers' Association, which held its last conference in 1971.

The consolidation of school districts was a severe setback to Island Acadians outside the Evangeline region, but it was offset to a degree by the decision of the federal government to promote bilingualism throughout Canada. The passage of the Official Languages Act in 1969 resulted in the establishment by the P.E.I. government of the Social Action Directorate to provide support to Acadian initiatives. Most notably, grants were provided to the St

Thomas Aquinas Society that allowed it to take on the role of cultural animator and lobbyist. The society's activities have included the promotion of francophone youth organizations, social animation activities in Acadian communities, the establishment of a French immersion program for teachers, and the publication of a French-language newspaper. In its role as lobbyist, the society succeeded in having the School Act amended in 1980 to give access to French education where numbers warrant it. As a consequence of this initiative, the French-language school board in the Evangeline region (which has the responsibility for French education for the whole province) initiated French-language classes in Charlottetown in September 1991 (A. Arsenault, personal communication, 25 Aug. 1991).

COMMUNITY CONTROL OF THE ECONOMY

A recent incident that is symbolic of the desire of the Evangeline community to control its own affairs, and the associated resistance to external forces, was the rejection of an initiative by McCain's, the large food processor. McCain's was considering the purchase of land in the Summerside area for industrial purposes. While other communities vied with one another to obtain a new McCain's plant, the sentiments in the Evangeline region communities were entirely the opposite. Instead of considering the actions they might take to attract McCain's, they were concerned with how they might prevent this corporate giant from buying land in their region (A. Arsenault, personal communication, 15 Aug. 1991). Faced with ongoing pressure from the anglophone majority to abandon their language and culture, the residents of Evangeline have learned that they must stand together to resist assimilation and to assert their identity. This attitude has been expressed not only with respect to matters of culture, where it is predominant, but also in economic affairs. The Evangeline people have understood that their aspirations for themselves and their children can only be achieved through a political process of struggle. Around the issue of culture, many Evangeline region people have connected the personal with the political and have developed a nationalist consciousness. This consciousness has expressed itself not only in opposition to assimilationist policies, but most characteristically in the creation of alternative organizations and the initiatives that these organizations have undertaken (for example, the Acadian Teachers' Association developing its own French curriculum).

With respect to economic issues, community control has been expressed very clearly in a long-standing co-operative tradition beginning with informal co-operation and eventually moving into an elaborate network of formally incorporated co-operatives. Informal co-operation in the Evangeline region predated the formation of co-operatives. Writing in 1924, historian Émile Lauvrière stated that the Acadian people practised a type of 'spontaneous communism' (182). This mutual aid, which took place primarily between relatives and neighbours, is described by Webster (1977) as 'people helping each other voluntarily to achieve mutually desired goals' (176). Necessary work for survival was accomplished through 'frolics' or 'work bees.' People gathered together to harvest their crops, cut and saw their lumber, spin their wool, or build houses, barns, and churches. These frolics combined business with pleasure. The day's work was followed by a shared meal and an evening of music and dance. Gallant argues that this tradition of mutual self-help, which used to exist between relatives and neighbours, explains in part the success of the Evangeline region co-operatives (C. Gallant 1982).

The beginnings of a more structured form of co-operation may be found in the seed grain banks, which sprang up in Acadian communities in the 1860s. In the Evangeline region , the first seed bank was initiated by the farmers of Egmont Bay in 1862. It was based on the ideas of Father Émile Belcourt, who in 1864 also initiated the Farmers' Bank of Rustico, a prototype of a credit union. The seed bank provided a mechanism for farmers to pool their resources so that everyone would have grain for spring seeding. The farmers belonging to the seed bank could borrow in the spring and pay back after harvest, with the interest paid in kind. This idea spread like wildfire, so that within a few years there were twenty-four seed banks. Interestingly enough, with one exception they were all in Acadian communities, something that did not go unnoticed by the editor of *The Examiner*, a Charlottetown newspaper, who, writing in 1868, praised this initiative effusively for its contribution to self-reliance: 'The Acadian French inhabitants of Egmont Bay have set our farmers an example of self-help and co-operative effort which they would do well to follow ... If such societies were established all over the Island, there would be no necessity for the Government to come to the assistance of a farming population of the Island even in the scarcest years' (2). A collectively-owned cheese factory established at Abram-Village in 1896 was the next experiment in co-operation. This time the stimulus came not from the local priest but from the federal government. Farmers were encouraged to form milk producers' associations for the purpose of constructing a cheese factory. In return for constructing the building and guaranteeing the supply of milk, the government undertook to produce and market the cheese, as well as pay rent on the building (Webster 1977). This cheese factory operated until 1952, when it amalgamated with other cheese-making associations to form Amalgamated Dairies of Summerside.

During the period 1890–1936, the federal government encouraged rural people to form a variety of agricultural clubs. It was thought that these associations would increase farmers' bargaining power and at the same time encourage the improvement of the quality and quantity of agricultural products. In the Evangeline region, the first agricultural club, formed in 1898, was intended to break the power of merchants and buyers by purchasing and selling collectively (C. Gallant 1982). Three years later, in 1901, the newly formed agricultural ministry of Prince Edward Island organized a system of Farmers' Institutes, which promoted a type of adult education for farming people. These Farmers' Institutes served as 'vehicle[s] for the improvement of seed, good livestock practices and the general transmission of innovations in agricultural technique' (Webster 1977, 80). In that same year, the farmers of the Evangeline area formed their own society under this system. Institute activities included general meetings three or four times a year with guest lectures on a variety of agricultural topics, discussion groups in people's homes twice a month, week-long courses on scientific agriculture, and a Farmers' Week in Charlottetown.

In addition to these educational activities, the Farmers' Institutes promoted the formation of a variety of agricultural clubs: animal breeding clubs to improve the quality of livestock; shipping clubs to improve the prices for farm merchandise; and buying clubs to reduce the cost of agricultural supplies. These were not formal co-operatives, in that they were not organized according to Rochdale principles, but they were similar in structure, that is, member-based mutual associations in which people voluntarily agreed to the joint ownership and use of breeding stock as well as joint buying and selling. In the Evangeline region there was a proliferation of clubs: breeding and shipping clubs for cattle, sheep, pigs, and horses; buying clubs for fertilizer, seed grain, and machinery; and even egg and poultry clubs. Indeed at the 1918 meeting of the Egmont Bay Farmers' Institute, the president, Edilbert Pouvier, credited the institutes for all the agricultural clubs that existed at that time in the parish (C. Gallant 1982).

In 1916, the Farmers' Institute of Egmont Bay decided to move beyond the temporary buying-club structure to set up a permanent co-operative store. Unfortunately this first experience with consumer co-operation was a failure and the store closed in 1926. There were several reasons for the store's failure: lack of co-operative legislation; insufficient capital and inexperienced managers; lack of co-operative education; and competition from established private operators. Perhaps most significant was the fact that the store sold on credit, rather than for cash.

While a large number of agricultural associations were formed in the Evangeline region between 1890 and 1920, it was not until 1931 and 1938 respectively that fishers' unions were established at Mont-Carmel and Egmont Bay. Webster (1977) explained this by citing the fishers' relatively dependent economic and social position. Unlike farmers, who at least owned their plot of land, many of the fishers owned nothing. A number worked as wage labourers for the buyers, who represented the fish companies. Even those who owned their own boats had no choice but to accept the prices offered by the buyers. According to historian J.T. Croteau: 'These large firms followed a practice of paying the fishermen the lowest prices for their catch, but of charging the top prices for their gear ... According to the usual custom the fisherman never knew at the beginning of the season just what he was going to receive for his fish. At the end of the season when he was paid off it was too late to protest ... The fisherman did not dare to say too much as he had to rely upon the packer for advances to carry himself and his family through the next winter' (1951, 85).

The situation began to change in 1924 with the organization of the first Fishermen's Union of Canada at Tignish. Due to the efforts of Chester McCarthy, the president of the Tignish union, legislation to provide for the organization of fishers' unions was put in place that same year. This was followed in 1927 by the McLean Royal Commission on fisheries in the Maritime provinces. This Commission, which stressed the importance of promoting co-operation among fishers, provided funds to establish a department of extension at St Francis Xavier University that would create adult education programs for fishers. In 1928, Father Moses Coady, the director of this new division and a leader of the Antigonish Movement, which spread rapidly throughout the Maritimes promoting co-operatives, was mandated by the federal minister of fisheries to organize fishers into co-operatives. In addition to the organization of fishers' unions, Coady and his people also organized study circles, credit unions, and co-operative stores.

In the Evangeline region, the first fishers' union, Mont-Carmel Fisheries Ltd, was incorporated in 1932. Though it had the organization of a co-operative, its legal form was that of a joint stock company. Both Chester McCarthy, the founder and manager of the Tignish Fishermen's Union, and Father Coady were involved in its formation. McCarthy held several informational meetings at Mont-Carmel, and the Mont-Carmel fishers visited Tignish to examine the union's operations. Father Coady also met with the fishers in the Evangeline village of Wellington in July 1931, at which time the union was formed. The Egmont Bay Fishermen's Union was not formed until 1938. Even though the Egmont Bay

fishers knew of the success of the fishers' unions at Tignish and
Mont-Carmel, they were deterred by the memory of the failed co-
operative store (C. Gallant 1982). In 1937 they were approached
by the former manager of the Mont-Carmel Union, who wished
to establish a second union. After considerable discussion fourteen fishers agreed to take this step. In 1938, members of the new
Egmont Bay Fishermen's Union constructed their own lobster
canning plant with the free labour of members, and supported by
a government loan. A year later they began selling their lobsters
directly to the American market. The increase in the returns they
received for their catch was dramatic. Instead of the nine cents
per pound offered by the buyers, they received from 17.5 to
19 cents per pound for large lobsters.

MODERN CO-OPERATION (1936–62)

The passing of the Credit Union Societies Act in 1936 and the Co-
operative Associations Act in 1938, based upon Rochdale principles, ushered in the modern era of co-operation. The year 1936
also saw the creation of the Prince Edward Island Adult Education League to introduce study circles to the Island. Popularized
by Father Coady and the Antigonish Movement, these clubs were
promoted in Prince Edward Island by Dr J.T. Croteau and the St
Dunstan's University Extension Service. Webster recounted that
these clubs 'were established on a neighbourly basis and people
were encouraged to question the forces that shaped their lives
and ponder what they could do to make needed changes' (1977,
187).

   In the Evangeline region, the study clubs were viewed as a
progression from the Farmers' Institutes. A variety of subjects
were studied: the Rochdale principles, the functioning of credit
unions, co-operative stores, rural electrification, and even the cat-
echism. The circles met weekly at the neighbourhood level, and
once monthly at the parish level. In addition, study circle members participated in week-long courses on co-operatives and
credit unions offered in the community by St Dunstan's. It is
interesting to note that in Wellington and Egmont Bay, the study

circles were composed entirely of men, while in Mont-Carmel women, men, and children attended the circles (C. Gallant 1982).

As a result of the study circles, the Evangeline region parishes quickly organized credit unions and co-operative stores. Dr Croteau of St Dunstan's, the priests, and a local leader, Cyrus Gallant, were prominent in the organization of the meetings that led to the formation of the three credit unions in 1937. As noted, the prototype of a credit union in Evangeline dated back to the 1860s when another priest, Father Belcourt, had founded the first people's bank in Canada. The lack of access to bank credit meant that the credit unions were successful from the start. Member participation was high. Volunteers visited each home at least once a month to pick up deposits, and general meetings were held on a monthly basis to make decisions. In addition to making individual loans, the credit unions also provided credit to co-operative organizations.

In 1970, on the recommendation of the Prince Edward Island Credit Union League, the three parish credit unions united to form the Evangeline Credit Union, located in Wellington. It commenced operations with 1,225 members and assets of $417,800. By 1990 the membership had increased to 2,500 and the assets to $5 million. Viewing itself as a social institution, the Evangeline Credit Union has taken an activist role in relation to both education and the economic development of the region. With respect to economic development, it contributed to employment creation by providing financing to commercial enterprises. In addition, it has also set up the Baie Acadienne Venture Capital Group to make available equity financing to new community enterprises.

While co-operative stores developed concurrently with the credit unions, their establishment was more problematic. It was not only that private stores already operated in the communities, but also that many people felt bound to the private merchants because they depended on their credit. Cyrus Gallant, himself a private merchant who had become an enthusiast of consumer co-operation, took the lead to organize community meetings and to promote the formation of a co-operative association. In 1937 the new co-operative association of Wellington rented his store and hired him as manager. In 1939, the co-operative opened four branch stores in surrounding communities. This expansion triggered a financial crisis that threatened the co-operative's survival. A succession of managers attempted to stabilize the business without success. In 1945 the directors requested Dr Croteau, now of the Co-op Union of Prince Edward Island, to study the financial management of the Wellington Co-operative Store. The study recommended increasing the share capital and decreasing the credit sales. In spite of these recommendations the store's financial situation did not improve, so the decision was taken to close the four branches. (After its branch store closed, the people of Mont-Carmel formed an association and opened their own store in 1949.)

Unfortunately the closing of the branch stores did not improve the financial position of the Wellington store. In 1958 it was again on the verge of bankruptcy. This time the co-operative was saved by a fire, which although it destroyed the building, allowed the association to pay off its debts with the insurance money. In October of the same year, the co-operative opened again in an old school building. With new policies to decrease credit sales, it began to operate successfully. The year 1964 saw the construction of a new store, and in 1971 there was an expansion. By 1971 it was on a solid financial footing with 412 members and sales of $1.1 million.

During this period the fishers' co-operatives in the Evangeline region also saw many changes. In 1944, both the Mont-Carmel and Egmont Bay fishers withdrew from the P.E.I. Fishermen's Union and joined the new P.E.I. Fishermen's Co-operative Central Association. In 1954 the two co-operatives joined together to sell their products in common. This worked so well that in 1955 the members voted to unite the two co-operatives to form the Acadian Co-operative Fishermen's Association. In 1964 the co-operative voted to accept members from outside the parishes of Mont-Carmel and Egmont Bay. Since the new members from the other side of the Island had licences to fish in the spring, while the Mont-Carmel and Egmont Bay fishers had licences to fish in the fall, the cannery could stay in production for a longer period.

On the downside, the increase in members led to fewer fisher assemblies and less participation in decisions by members.

Toward the end of the 1960s the idea of building a new cannery surfaced. A desire to increase production and the need for a refrigerated warehouse were motivating factors. The question was discussed at a members' meeting in 1969, attended by the minister of fisheries of P.E.I. and representatives from the Department of Extension of the University of St Dunstan's. In addition the federal government and the Union of Maritime Fishermen (UMF) were also involved in the discussions. Finally, in 1970, the members voted to construct a new cannery estimated to cost $750,000. The cost was divided between the co-operative and the federal government, with the province providing a loan guarantee, and UMF investing $450,000.

Opened in 1971, the new cannery has been plagued with financial problems. Since the quantity of fish has decreased, the plant is too large. In 1982, as a result of a $2 million debt, additional loans from the UMF were needed if the co-operative was to survive. This outside involvement, according to C. Gallant, 'has resulted in a lack of interest in the fishermen who have lost to a certain extent control of their organization' (1982, 197).

Another co-operative formed during this period was the Farmers' Marketing Co-operative. During the period 1937–55 farmers had sold their potatoes through the Wellington Co-operative Store. As the interests of producers and consumers conflicted to a certain extent, the farmers formed their own co-operative in 1955. In addition to pooling and selling potatoes, the co-operative operated a feed mill and rented out implements for planting and harvesting. Although it was financially successful, the need for this co-operative declined as the number of farmers decreased. This trend was accelerated by the P.E.I. Development Plan of 1969, which assisted marginal farmers to move off the land. This co-operative was dissolved in 1972.

THE NEW CO-OPERATIVES (1962–PRESENT)

Influenced by the Antigonish Movement, many Maritime communities formed fishers' co-operatives, credit unions, and co-operative stores during the 1930s and 40s, but in most communities the formation of new co-operatives as a means of community economic development has not continued. The Evangeline region of Prince Edward Island is one of the striking exceptions. After a period of consolidation in the 1950s, the people of the Evangeline region formed three co-operatives between 1962 and 1973 and fourteen co-operatives since 1977 (C. McNeill, 1977; personal communication, 22 Aug. 1991). The intent of Antigonish Movement co-operatives was to reduce the exploitation of farmers and fishers at the hands of merchants, buyers, and banks by establishing mutual self-help institutions to provide these services. The new co-operatives have additional objectives, the primary one being that of community economic development through employment creation. Of the new Evangeline co-operatives, six provide services to members of the region, seven deal primarily with the creation of employment, and four are for educational purposes, culture, and technical support.

The new Evangeline region service co-operatives include two for housing, and one each for health care, nursing care, cable television, and funeral services. The first housing co-operative, Acadian Housing, was formed in 1963 at the instigation of Roger Arsenault, who arranged a meeting between the P.E.I. Housing Commission and interested Evangeline region residents. Those who wished to build their own houses collectively formed a study group that met during the winter of 1962–3. A loan of $34,400 to build the six houses was arranged through Central Mortgage and Housing Corporation (now Canada Mortgage and Housing Corporation), the federal agency responsible for housing policy. A local person was hired to supervise the work and construction started on 15 July 1963. While basements, plumbing, and electrical wiring were contracted out, all other work was completed by the members themselves. Their method was to work from six to ten o'clock at night from Monday to Friday. Occasionally the relatives of the members would organize a 'frolic' to speed the work along. On one such night twenty persons came to help install insulation in the house of Roger

Arsenault. After the work was finished everyone enjoyed a 'fricot' (clam stew) before going home (C. Gallant 1982). By the summer of 1964, the houses were completed and the families moved in. As a result of the joint efforts, the cost of each house was only $6,000.

The Evangeline Health Care Co-operative was founded in 1977 to provide bilingual medical services within the region. Ernest Arsenault submitted the idea to the annual meeting of the village of Wellington. A committee representing the three parishes was formed, which held a public meeting to found the co-operative.

The Community Communications Co-operative was formed in 1985 after the community learned that a Nova Scotia company had requested permission from the Canadian Radio-television and Telecommunications Commission (CRTC) to establish a cable system in the Evangeline region. A group of residents who opposed the plan organized a community-controlled cable system to ensure that French language stations would be available to Evangeline region residents (P. Gallant, personal communication, 25 Aug. 1991). In 1988 a second housing co-operative, Gabriel Housing, was organized by the Evangeline Co-operative Council to provide co-operative housing to residents who could not afford to own their own homes.

The fifth service co-operative, the Evangeline Funeral Co-operative, was formed in 1986. Initiated by Leo Arsenault, it operates with volunteers and has reduced the cost of funerals by thirty per cent (L. Arsenault, personal communication, 24 Aug. 1991). Chez Nous, a nursing-care co-operative founded in 1992 by five local women, offers accommodation and care to twenty-five of the region's senior citizens (J. Laforest, 16 Sept. 1992).

The direct use of co-operatives to create employment marks a departure from the Antigonish Movement model, which had emphasized provision of services to residents of the region. As might be expected this move has been accompanied by both successes and failures. Of the seven employment co-operatives that were formed, three have closed, while four have survived. In terms of ownership and control, four of the seven were structured as traditional co-operatives with community ownership and hired workers, while three were structured as worker co-operatives, with ownership limited to workers.

Le Village, a community co-operative that provides employment based on tourism, had its origins in 1966 at a community meeting to identify a winter-works project. It had been a bad year for fishing, so desperate fishers were looking for a way to get through the winter. This development started with the construction of an Acadian Pioneer Village. It now includes a restaurant, motel, dinner theatre, handicraft shop, conference centre, and tour company (A. Gallant, personal communication, 26 Aug. 1992). Currently it employs some 85 persons, although most positions are seasonal.

The second employment-oriented co-operative was a handicraft co-operative. It was formed by Jacqueline Arsenault and other women from Abram-Village who had attended handicraft classes and had decided to produce articles for sale. In the first few years, they operated as a guild, but in 1973 incorporated as a co-operative and built their own store (J. Arsenault, personal communication, 24 Aug. 1991).

In 1978, the first worker co-operative on the Island, Acadian Co-operative Enterprises, was formed. The co-operative planned to raise rabbits on a commercial basis and to manufacture articles from fur. Funding for the start-up came from a Canada Employment program, so that the co-operative had to adhere to a number of regulations that hindered its flexibility. In particular, the ruling that workers must come from the chronically unemployed meant that the co-operative was unable to select members on the basis of their experience and skills. When the Local Employment Assistance Program grant from Employment and Immigration Canada ran out in 1982, the co-operative had not become self-sustaining and it was dissolved (C. Gallant 1982).

As a result of provincial initiative in 1979 to promote clearing and reforestation, the Acadian Industrial Commission hired consultants to study the possibility of a forest industry. The consultants' report was discussed at a public meeting in 1980. As a consequence of public interest, a forestry co-operative was soon formed to produce wood chips. An adequate market could not be found so this co-operative too was dissolved (C. Gallant 1982).

A second craft co-operative, this time specializing in wooden products, was organized in 1985. Situated on the edge of the Evangeline region, this co-operative was initiated by the mixed Acadian/English parish of Richmond/Wellington and the non-governmental organization Plura.

In 1986 another worker-owned business, the P.E.I. Potato Chip Co-operative, was formed. The idea of producing potato chips arose out of a series of 'kitchen meetings' to discuss the employment needs of the region. The technical studies, financing, and organizing of the co-operative was arranged by the Evangeline Co-operative Council with the help of the Baie Acadienne Venture Capital Group. This co-operative ran into financial difficulties, and after attempts at restructuring, was sold to an Ontario firm in 1993. Also in 1986, Les P'tits Acadiens, a worker co-operative to manufacture children's clothing, came into being. It too had difficulty marketing its products at a price that provided an adequate return to workers, and closed in 1990 (A. Arsenault, personal communication, 19 Feb. 1991).

In addition to the service and employment co-operatives, there is an arts co-operative, which offers courses and lessons in music and dance; a school co-operative run by students themselves, which operates a canteen and sells school supplies to student members; and an international development co-operative, which operates twinning projects in conjunction with co-operatives in Haiti. Most important of this group is the Co-operative Council, a second-tier development co-operative to which each of the primary co-operatives in the region belong. The Co-operative Council encourages the individual co-operatives to think in terms of the overall welfare of the region (C. McNeill, personal communication, 28 Aug. 1991).

CONCLUSION

The evidence suggests that the Evangeline region of Prince Edward Island has created an innovative approach, which utilizes co-operatives for community economic development. Essentially the residents of the region have taken the initiative to create an interrelated network of co-operatives that provide basic services. This approach to community economic development has come about primarily during the past twenty years, but also is rooted in the traditions of the community. In order to understand the process through which new ventures are formed, we have selected four to study in depth. Two of the cases were service co-operatives with a broad community membership, which are most typical of the pattern in the region, and two others were worker co-operatives with membership limited to the workers of these enterprises. The worker co-operatives also differed in that they were oriented primarily to a market that was outside the region, whereas the service co-operatives served the residents of Evangeline. All four were started since the mid-1980s, and therefore were ripe for analysis when the study was conducted in 1992. The cases were studied through a combination of participant observation, in-depth interviews with key participants, and document analyses. (For details of the research method, see appendix.) Following a narrative account of the formation of the four co-operatives (chapter 2), the critical factors associated with formation are discussed (chapter 3), and subsequently (chapter 4) a theoretical framework is presented to explain the essential elements of community economic development. In the final chapter (chapter 5), the implications for practice and policy are discussed.

2
Four Case Histories

I think co-ops are formed because there's a need. There's something
missing and you have to do something about it. And people just start
talking and get together, and all of a sudden it develops into a committee ... This first idea is not that we're going to form a co-operative. It just
moves into that spirit after a while.
Evangeline resident

This chapter contains case histories of the development of four
Evangeline region co-operatives, all initiated since 1985. Chez
Nous and the Community Communications Co-operative, with
community-wide memberships, were organized to provide services to the community. The Prince Edward Island Potato Chip
Co-operative and Les P'tits Acadiens, with membership limited
to workers, were created to provide employment through the
production of goods for sale outside the region. The case histories
that follow tell the stories of the co-operatives' formation, the
support they received, and the difficulties they faced. The case
histories are based upon interviews with key participants, analyses of important documents, and participant observation. Following the case histories is an analysis of the factors in common that
led to the formation of these co-operatives, with a view to developing a model of community economic development.

LE CHEZ NOUS CO-OPERATIVE

At a special community meeting on 16 September 1992, Lorraine

Arsenault, president of Chez Nous Co-operative, a community-based service co-operative, triumphantly announced the results of a secret ballot that had just been held. By a large margin, the members had voted to proceed immediately with the construction of a community-care centre for Evangeline region seniors. This decision marked the culmination of almost two years of effort by Lorraine and her planning committee.

With the overwhelming support of community members and community organizations in the Evangeline region, this new co-operative had mounted a fund-raising campaign that within two years raised more than $110,000 in cash and pledges. Using this evidence of community support as leverage, the co-operative had successfully negotiated with outside public and private agencies for supplementary financing assistance. As a result, Lorraine announced to the meeting that in addition to a previous commitment of $122,000 from Canada Employment and Immigration, she had just received a telephone message that the Fisheries Alternative Program of the Atlantic Canada Opportunities Agency had awarded Chez Nous a further grant of $100,000. In more good news, Lorraine reported that L'Assomption Assurance, an Acadian company based in New Brunswick, had not only pledged a donation of $10,000 but had also agreed to provide a mortgage at a reduced rate of interest. She pointed out that taken together these commitments amounted to well over 50 per cent of the total construction costs of $550,000 (J. Laforest, 16 Sept. 1992). With the green light given by the community meeting, the initiators were able to pursue their dream of building a facility to provide community care to Acadian seniors in their own language. When Chez Nous opened in March 1993, this dream became a reality.

Background

The need for such a community-care facility had been identified in 1985 after a local entrepreneur requested the provincially funded Regional Services Centre to conduct a survey to assess the need. The provincial Ministry of Health and Social Services hired a local nurse to prepare a questionnaire and carry out the study. This survey, which included fifty senior citizens, as well as the presidents of municipal councils, parish councils, and senior citizens' organizations, took place early in 1986 (R. Arsenault, 11 Dec. 1985). Although the results indicated a great need for a centre that would offer elementary nursing services, no action was taken (R. Arsenault, 19 Feb. 1986a). The idea was resurrected in 1988 at the annual meeting of the Evangeline Health Care Co-operative. Since a number of members indicated interest in such a project, the board of directors was instructed to pursue discussions with representatives of the Co-operative Council and the Regional Services Centre. Again the matter was dropped (R. Arsenault, 30 Mar. 1988).

It was not until 1991 that a determined effort was made to organize a community-care facility. This time the impetus came from the painful experiences of two local women – Louise Arsenault and Lorraine Arsenault. When Louise's mother was stricken with Alzheimer's disease, it had been necessary to put her in a community-care facility in Summerside. Also when her mother-in-law reached age ninety, Louise was no longer able to care for her, so she too had to go to Summerside. According to Louise, they were very lonely there since 'it was all English people and strangers to them.'

Lorraine had been a nursing attendant for many years at the manor in Summerside. She knew the problems and the heartache that resulted from moving Acadian seniors from their homes to an English milieu. She recalled one episode where an older French woman was upset during the night and called for an attendant. When the attendant came out of the woman's room, she said to Lorraine: 'Why don't you build a nursing home out in Egmont Bay and take all these old French people home with you?' This incident affected Lorraine profoundly. She decided that some day she would do it!

A few years later, she started looking after old people on a private-patient basis. Sometimes she would take them to her home, which meant she was responsible twenty-four hours a day. Although she loved to do it, she found that the provision of total care was too much for her. She began to think about buying a big house where she could look after four or five seniors with the help of a small hired staff. One day when she and Louise were out driving, she noticed a For Sale sign on a vacant school. Louise asked: 'Why don't we buy it and fix it up and take in these old people who are still able to look after themselves?' 'You know, that's an idea,' Lorraine replied. 'Let's try it just for fun.'

Since the property was owned by the Evangeline Credit Union, the women went there first to enquire about the price. Next they decided to talk to others who might be able to help them. At this point they were thinking of renovating the old school so their group could be licensed as a community-care facility for perhaps ten senior citizens. The first person they approached was Jeanita Bernard, the local home-care supervisor for the Department of Health and Social Services. She suggested that they meet with Amand Arsenault, director of the Regional Service Centre and an employee of the Department of Community and Cultural Affairs. Arsenault responded enthusiastically to their idea. He obtained the key to the repossessed building and went with the women to look at it. He also arranged for an employee of the Prince Edward Island Housing Corporation to come along. This person agreed to prepare preliminary sketches for a renovation, along with cost projections. Unfortunately the costs projections were alarmingly high.

Since renovating the old schoolhouse was impractical, the women came up with the idea of constructing a new building. Among the people they met with was Leonce Bernard, the local M.L.A., who strongly encouraged them to proceed with the construction of a new facility. He informed them that there were resource persons available in government to help them; that such a facility had been needed in the community for twenty years; and that previous groups had tried but been discouraged by the amount of work involved. 'Go ahead,' he said, 'and when the going gets tough, don't quit.'

Building the Volunteer Group

On Amand's suggestion Lorraine and Louise sought out other

interested people. The first person they contacted was Ida Gallant, president of the Evangeline Health Care Co-operative. An active volunteer in many community projects, she joined eagerly, telling them she had wanted such a facility for a long time. Two younger women were contacted next, who had little organizing experience but who had training in resident care and were looking for employment. At this point the initiators were thinking of operating the seniors' home as a five-person worker co-operative. The younger women would be paid employees, and the three older women would work as volunteers.

As this group of five continued to meet, they began to realize that they needed the total support of the community if they were to succeed. They wondered whether they would receive this support if they structured the project as a worker co-operative with part of the surplus returning to themselves. This forced them to think more carefully about their purpose. It became clear to them that above all else they wanted to look after their senior citizens. Making money so that they could give rebates to the worker-owners was very much a secondary consideration. In Lorraine's words: 'It's not to make money ... The money is just to be able to look after those people and to pay the people that would be working there.' Out of this struggle to define their purpose, they came to the conclusion that the worker co-operative model would not meet their needs. Instead they required a model that would attract the broadest community support. Starting a co-operative with wide community membership seemed to meet this requirement, so they shifted their ideas in that direction.

Things now began to move quickly. Amand Arsenault suggested that they involve more people, especially those with special skills or previous experience in organizing such a project. He reported that when the P.E.I. Potato Chip Co-operative started, the work had been divided among five committees: Land and Building, Finance, Personnel, Fund-raising, and By-laws and Regulations. Deciding to follow this pattern, the initiating group drew up a list of people to contact. In making their selection they considered criteria such as reliability, the necessity for representation from every community in the Evangeline region, and relevant knowledge and experience. For the By-laws and Regulations Committee, they selected Claudette McNeill of the Co-operative Council and Alcide Bernard of the P.E.I. Potato Chip Co-operative because they were knowledgeable in this area; for the Land and Building Committee, they chose carpenters from the community; for the Personnel Committee they identified the manager of L'Étoile restaurant; and for the Finance Committee they decided to approach persons who worked at the Evangeline Credit Union. Once they had prepared the list, each of the five initiators agreed to approach three people to ascertain their willingness to serve on the committees. To their great satisfaction, not one person who was approached refused to participate!

On 24 July 1991 the initiators of Chez Nous Co-operative held a public meeting and press conference to explain their plans to the community and to enlist support. At the meeting, which was attended by some fifty residents, they stated their intention to construct a community-care centre to accommodate twenty-five seniors from the area who were not able to live alone but did not yet require nursing-home care. The cost of this centre would be in the neighbourhood of $420,000 (Père Noel, 7 Aug. 1991). Shortly after the meeting, the initiating group received an offer that could have taken all the work off their hands. An operator of community-care centres in other parts of the Island, who had asked a local contractor to prepare a sketch of such a facility, to be situated in Abram-Village, requested permission to attend a meeting of Chez Nous to present his proposed plan. The group discussed the offer, but decided not to invite the entrepreneur to their meeting. They felt it was important for the community to have control over such a centre so that it could be planned to meet the unique needs of Evangeline region seniors. Ida explained it this way: 'We want the control. That's why we didn't want an outsider to come in. We wanted a co-operative so we can set the price according to what it's going to cost. We want to be able to adjust the price to fit these people who have only a small pension from the government. If there had been an outside company that took over, we wouldn't have any say in it.' In addition they wanted to be able to ensure that the establishment would employ local workers, and that the main language of the business would be French. As Lorraine put it, 'They'd be taking our money out. We want to keep our money here. God only knows that the Evangeline region is not that rich.' In their opinion, not only would a development by an outsider not meet their needs, it simply would not work. At the monthly rates of $1,400–$1,500 that this individual charged in his other centres, most Evangeline seniors would be unable to use the facility.

After the public meeting in July, the Fund-Raising Committee of Chez Nous swung into high gear. Someone had jokingly asked Lorraine if she expected to find the building in her Christmas stocking. Her response was 'Hey, you think that's funny? I'm going to push that!' So the committee held a fund-raiser on 24 August called Christmas in August. This event, which included a rocking chair 'rockathon' for pledges, raised $8,000. About this time Chez Nous received another big boost when a local resident donated three acres of land as a building site. Located in the village of Wellington beside the health care co-operative, the site was ideal.

The Fund-Raising Committee then organized event after event. They solicited cooked food from the community and sold meals at the Atlantic Violinists' Jubilee and the Acadian Festival. They arranged fun nights at the Legion, where they auctioned off donated prizes. They held lotteries, draws, and a bikeathon from Tignish to the other end of Prince Edward Island. Finally, on 6 June 1992, they held a celebrity auction. One of the two hundred articles donated for sale was Brian Mulroney's tie (Laforest, 1 July 1992).

Not to be outdone, community members and organizations also started to raise money. A local garage raffled off a large bottle of liquor and donated the proceeds. The parishes organized a series of four benefit concerts, some of which were attended by four or five hundred people. At these concerts, which raised as much as $2,000 in a single afternoon, people made contributions not only at the door but throughout the afternoon as the hat was passed around. One of the priests, an excellent musician, personally organized an afternoon of singing and dancing from his own extended family. The municipalities also got involved with a pot-luck supper and a bingo to raise money for Chez Nous.

Donations and pledges started flowing in apart from specific fund-raising events. The donations were both financial and otherwise. A local contractor promised to donate a number of hours of labour; the two local M.L.A.'s contributed a quarter of beef for one of the lotteries; a local craftsperson donated a beautiful handmade quilt. Seniors in the community were also supportive. Some who thought they might later need the service contributed a down payment of their first month's rent. One person gave a thousand dollars and pledged a thousand every six months for up to three years.

Evangeline region community organizations were particularly generous. The Legion pledged $2,000 a year for five years, while the Legion Auxiliary pledged $1,200 a year for the same period. The co-operative store pledged $1,000, the credit union $5,000 and the funeral co-operative $1,000. All in all the fund-raising campaign was so successful that by the time of the celebrity auction on 6 June 1992, the committee had exceeded its target of $70,000. Amand, who had been involved in many community projects, marvelled at the support for Chez Nous: 'There have been co-operative community projects in the past. And you have your interest groups and people who are supportive and people who are indifferent. But this project ... Everybody's come to rally around this project. It's unreal!'

Meanwhile the project was receiving help from community leaders and resource people from both within and outside the community. Once the fund-raising campaign had been launched, the initiating group began to survey seniors to find out how many were prepared to make a commitment to use the facility. The idea had been suggested to them by a resource person from the Division of Aging, Department of Health and Social Services. This person also made suggestions about the design of the facilities, helped them prepare a profile sheet to gather information, and went with them for the first few meetings with seniors. Claudette McNeill, the co-ordinator of the Co-operative Council, and Alcide Bernard, the manager of the P.E.I. Potato Chip Co-operative, helped them decide upon the structure of the co-operative and performed the detailed task of drawing up the by-laws and arranging for incorporation. According to the initiators, Claudette 'provided guidance about how to go about things.'

This expert knowledge about how to get things done became particularly important when Chez Nous, a non-profit organization, tried to obtain a charitable tax number. At first Revenue Canada refused to consider a tax number for a co-operatively structured organization. This precipitated a crisis for Chez Nous, to the point that the initiators decided to dissolve the co-operative and to set up a non-profit company. However, Claudette was able to arrange for the Conseil canadien de la coopération (CCC), the apex organization for francophone co-operatives in Canada, to lobby on behalf of Chez Nous. This intervention by the CCC was successful, with the result that a tax number was granted in the nick of time.

According to the initiators themselves, the most significant resource person of all was Amand Arsenault. He was not only director of the Regional Services Centre, but also a trusted community leader active in a variety of projects. They came to him initially to discuss their idea, and it was he who worked in an ongoing way as a consultant to their group. In addition to the developmental assistance he provided, he was also able to help the group to access outside resource persons. One of these was a planner from the provincial Community and Cultural Affairs Department, who prepared preliminary sketches and who worked on the transfer of the title to the land. On another occasion Amand enabled the group to obtain a grant to hire their own co-ordinator, Antoine Richard, from the Department of Community and Cultural Affairs' Co-operative Development Fund. Once the co-ordinator was hired, Amand, through his department, was able to provide him with office space, telephone, and secretarial support.

With the hiring of Antoine, a community leader and retired federal civil servant, as project co-ordinator, the capacity of Chez Nous to access outside resources increased dramatically. An application for an employment-creation grant through Canada

Employment and Immigration was submitted and eventually approved. This Section 25 grant of $121,000 would cover most of the labour costs involved in construction. The groundwork for the creation of a foundation was completed. A proposal to the Fisheries Alternative Program of the Atlantic Canada Opportunities Agency was prepared. Also, L'Assomption Assurance of New Brunswick was contacted, and a donation of $10,000 obtained.

Planning for Viability

While activities of the Fund-Raising Committee received the most attention from the fall of 1991 to the spring of 1992, other committees were working quietly behind the scenes. The Land and Building Committee had devised an innovative plan to save on architectural fees. As two young persons from the Evangeline region were studying architectural drafting at Summerside's Holland College, the committee arranged for their class to develop the blueprints for the Chez Nous building. Instead of the original architect's estimate of $40,000, the blueprints cost only $2,000. Lorraine described this as 'trying to do it ourselves. We're trying to put the building up community-wise, not architectural-wise.' With the blueprints finalized, the committee was able to obtain price quotes from contractors.

The Finance Committee also became active by April 1992. While they felt confident that Chez Nous had sufficient equity to obtain a mortgage and proceed with construction, they were concerned about operating costs. Since most Evangeline region seniors were not in a position to pay more than $800 to $850 per month, the committee had to find a way to either lower or in some way subsidize the rental costs. With the energetic assistance of their co-ordinator they explored a number of avenues. One of these was a submission for grant assistance to the Fisheries Alternative Program of the Atlantic Canada Opportunities Agency. It was thought that Chez Nous would qualify as a project generating sustainable employment in the community. Another was the initiation of negotiations with L'Assomption Assurance to provide Chez Nous with a mortgage at a reduced interest rate. A further avenue was the creation of a foundation with tax-exempt status as a fund-raising mechanism to access corporations in Prince Edward Island and other French organizations outside the province.

On 1 July 1992, the Chez Nous Co-operative held another public meeting to decide whether to proceed with construction or to delay until the co-operative was able to raise additional funds. A financial report was presented. The Fund-Raising Committee had amassed a total of $73,131.59. In addition, the Section 25 grant from Employment and Immigration guaranteed $121,000. As a result the $544,000 building could be constructed with a mortgage of $350,000. As well, the costs of the annual operation of Chez Nous were estimated to be $238,540, which included staff salaries of $133,000. Based on these projections, and an eighty per cent occupancy rate, the co-operative would have to charge each senior $952 per month.

At this point a vigorous debate ensued. Some felt that construction should go ahead, whereas others pointed out that the $952 figure was still too high for many seniors. One of the considerations pushing for an affirmative decision was a condition attached to the Section 25 grant from Employment and Immigration Canada: In order to retain the funding, construction had to begin before the end of March 1993. Given Prince Edward Island's weather, this meant that actual construction must commence no later than October 1992, so the structure could be enclosed before the winter storms.

After a good deal of discussion, the decision was postponed, and the officers of Chez Nous were encouraged to pursue their efforts during the summer. There would be a meeting in September to make a final decision. To the five women who started Chez Nous, this was a disappointment. It was now two years since they had started the project. At the beginning they had thought it would take only six months. And yet they knew their plans had to be laid carefully if the co-operative was to succeed. Ida put it this way: 'You have to be sure that once you get the building done and the people in it, you have some way of running it.'

At the follow-up meeting on 16 September 1992, the disappointment of the initiating group changed to elation. Thanks to the efforts of the co-ordinator and the Finance Committee many good things had happened since July: the grant from the Fisheries Alternative Program had been approved; L'Assomption Assurance had agreed to favourable mortgage terms; and the funeral co-operative had donated an additional $21,000. As a result, the projected monthly charge to seniors could be reduced to $870. With all this positive news, the consensus of the meeting was to proceed immediately with construction.

Thinking about all that had taken place since the Fund-Raising Committee had organized the Christmas in August event one year before, Lorraine said, 'Last year having the home for Christmas was a dream ... a beautiful dream. But this year it could be a reality.'

THE COMMUNITY COMMUNICATIONS CO-OPERATIVE

On 4 December 1985, Roger Gallant, president of the Community Communications Co-operative, with Ken MacLean, president of the Prince Edward Island Co-operative Union, looking on, signed the papers to officially incorporate the new co-operative. At that time Roger stated that the co-operative expected to receive permission from the Canadian Radio-television and Telecommunications Commission (CRTC) to operate a cable television system in the region by January or February 1986. As soon as the CRTC granted permission, the plan was for the co-operative to purchase the necessary equipment and proceed with the installation of cable. He indicated as well that in the first year of operation cable service would be available only in the most populated areas: Abram-Village, Wellington, and Urbainville (R. Arsenault, 4 Dec. 1985). In the second year the co-operative hoped to extend the service, so that by the end of the third year the whole region would be covered. The new cable system would bring in eight television stations, of which two or three would be French-language, and one would be a community station (R. Arsenault, 21 Aug. 1985).

The beginnings of this co-operative can be traced to a 1985 proposal by M1 Rural Television and Cable Systems to bring cable
television to eighty-seven small core-market communities in
Newfoundland, Nova Scotia, and Prince Edward Island ('M1
Rural,' 5 Sept. 1985). At precisely that time, Darlene Arsenault, a
communications officer with the St Thomas Aquinas Society of
P.E.I., was in contact with Canadian Satellite Communication Inc.
(CANCOM) to investigate the possibility of obtaining cable television for the Evangeline region. Officials of CANCOM informed
her about M1 Rural Television and Cable System's application to
the CRTC for a licence to establish a cable system in the two most
populated of the Evangeline villages. At first Darlene was excited
about the extra stations, but she quickly began to have second
thoughts. M1 Rural's application showed that it had no intention
of taking into account the distinctive character and needs of the
region. According to the M1 Rural proposal, the region would
receive seven channels, all of them English-language. Also there
was no provision for a community channel or for subsequent
expansion to the more sparsely populated areas. Darlene expressed her concerns: 'At first it seemed to be good news, but
then we thought our community is not just Abram-Village and
Wellington. We had Cap-Egmont and Mont-Carmel, and there
was no talk of expansion or anything ... If you have a big corporation coming in, they feed you any kind of channels that they want
and not what you want to watch. And no French channels! And
there wouldn't be any community channels. It would be like a
foreign occupation force coming into the community, bombard-
ing it with English channels and taking over the main centres of
Abram-Village and Wellington.'

Involving the Community

Darlene wasted no time sharing this information with the community. First, she approached Claudette McNeill, the manager of
the Co-operative Council. Claudette's response was that they
should 'gather up a few people around the table to see what they
think.' Together, they spread the news to representatives of the

primary community organizations and other community activists. They organized meetings at which M1 Rural's plans were discussed. After two or three such meetings a working committee was formed to organize community opposition to M1 Rural's proposal.

The concerns about M1 Rural's proposal were presented publicly by the Co-operative Council at its May 1985 annual meeting, attended by some sixty people. The council not only voted to oppose M1 Rural's application, but also agreed to send a letter of intervention to the CRTC indicating the region's displeasure. In addition, the council decided to survey the region to find out how many people were interested in having cable TV. If the number was sufficient, the council would consider the formation of a co-operative system in the villages of Wellington, Urbainville, and Abram-Village. This would keep the profits in the region, and later on the system could be expanded to the other villages. The proposed cable co-operative would create a significant amount of local employment through the installation, hook-ups, maintenance of equipment, and administration. It was noted as well that the co-operative would keep open the possibility of the community eventually having its own station for local broadcasts.

A letter was sent to all the organizations in the Evangeline region, asking them to submit briefs to the CRTC opposing M1 Rural's application. The many problems with the application were pointed out, including 'anglicising the Acadian population more than it is already' (R. Arsenault, 12 June 1985). Instead the letter called for the formation of a cable co-operative that would serve the whole region. Since the co-operative would not be concerned about profits to shareholders, it was argued, all the revenues from the enterprise could be re-invested, so that eventually the whole community might have access to cable.

In addition to requesting organizations to submit briefs, the working committee also prepared protest forms for individuals to sign and send directly to the CRTC. With the financial assistance of the St Thomas Aquinas Society and the backing of the Evangeline residents, Darlene travelled to Gander, Newfoundland, to present a brief on 26 June opposing M1 Rural's application. As a result of this intervention, the CRTC refused to grant M1 Rural a cable licence for the Evangeline region.

The way was now open for the Evangeline region to make its own application. Nineteen Evangeline region organizations submitted briefs to the CRTC in support of the cable co-operative's licence application, and one opposed it. The Baie Acadienne Industrial Commission and the Evangeline Arts Council, two of those who supported the co-operative in an unqualified way, cited the positive impact on the economy, the importance of access to additional French-language channels, and the learning opportunities for artists that a community channel would provide. Some of the other organizations who indicated their support were the municipal councils of Wellington and Abram-Village, the Unit 5 School Board, and the Acadian Committee for the Evangeline region.

The very influential St Thomas Aquinas Society, while indicating support, wanted assurance that several of the new channels would be in the French language. Its brief explained that presently Evangeline region youth principally watched English broadcasts, so that they were gradually becoming more comfortable in English than in French. As a result the Evangeline region population, which represents forty-one per cent of the francophones in P.E.I., was in the process of assimilation. The task of the cable co-operative would be to remedy this situation by bringing in the new French stations that were not available by satellite. With respect to the proposed community channel, the St Thomas Aquinas Society supported it as long as the community channel adopted policies that would ensure 80 to 90 per cent French-language programming. Like other organizations supporting the project, the St Thomas Aquinas Society underlined the important contribution that the new co-operative would make to the economy.

The Acadian newspaper, *La Voix Acadienne*, also supported the project, with reservations. In a letter sent to the co-operative, the newspaper deplored the amount of energy being spent on obtaining a cable distribution system, which would bring in additional English-language stations. Television, *La Voix* argued, posed the greatest threat to the assimilation of Acadian people.

The District 5 Teachers' Association submitted a brief that opposed the project outright. They, too, feared the impact of the six new anglophone channels on the region's Acadians. Their brief pointed out that many students came to classes with a weak knowledge of their mother tongue, because they watched English-language television. The Teachers' Association feared that the cable co-operative's programming would increase the trend to anglicization (R. Arsenault, 19 Feb. 1986b).

In spite of the reservations of a minority of Evangeline region organizations, the CRTC approved the cable co-operative's licence application in April 1986. The co-operative would access eight channels, of which three – Quatre Saisons, TCTV of Montreal, and CBAFT of Moncton – were French-language stations. Financial details included with the application revealed that the cost of the necessary satellite dish would be $22,000, while the cable installation would cost $10,000 per mile. The total cost of the first stage of the project was estimated at $100,000. With each subscriber paying $20 per month, in addition to the $50 membership fee, the projected income of $32,000 per year would enable the co-operative to operate on a profitable basis (R. Arsenault, 12 June 1985).

Preparing the Service

Once the licence was approved in April 1986, preparations moved into high gear. Community meetings were held to disseminate information and to encourage the purchase of shares. According to Claudette McNeill, the Co-operative Council played an active role in this process: 'The council kind of took that on; the responsibility of getting it set up and getting the members.' In June, the council applied for and obtained project funding from Employment and Immigration Canada to hire a local student to do a telephone survey of the 251 residences eligible for hook-up in order to identify those interested in subscribing to cable. At this time the co-operative also decided to hire a professional firm to prepare an overall plan for cable distribution and to recommend the appropriate equipment.

In the last week of September 1986, Roger Gallant, the president of the provisional committee of the co-operative, called a special meeting at the Evangeline Educational Centre. He reported that the co-operative had begun to make the technical plans necessary for installation of the system. Also financial arrangements to cover the cost of purchasing and installing the equipment had been negotiated. Subject to the cable co-operative's raising $9,500 from the sale of shares, the Evangeline Credit Union was prepared to lend $40,000, while the Baie Acadienne Venture Capital Group (the venture capital company started by the credit union) was prepared to invest $48,000. Roger reported, however, that the sale of membership shares had been much lower than anticipated. While 150 to 170 member-subscribers were required, only 28 persons had purchased shares. Roger noted that there appeared to be a decline in interest in the cable co-operative among residents of Evangeline. Whereas a survey of 270 residences conducted in the summer of 1985 had indicated that 70 per cent of those eligible were interested in membership, the most recent survey showed that interest had fallen to 35 to 45 per cent. As a result, the project was up in the air. Unless the necessary number of shares could be sold, the project might have to be dropped. It was felt that residents were unwilling to purchase shares because they didn't have enough information about the services being offered. Consequently the co-operative decided to hire someone to visit people in their homes to explain the services and encourage them to join (R. Arsenault, 30 Apr. 1986).

By mid-November, just five weeks later, the situation had changed dramatically. Ninety-four additional memberships had been sold, which brought the total to 122. Although the Evangeline Credit Union had originally insisted on a minimum of 150 member-subscribers as a condition of the loan, the cable co-operative's board of directors had now obtained agreement from the credit union to accept a minimum of 120 (R. Arsenault, 22 Oct. 1986). With this assurance, the board of directors decided to proceed. The president informed the press that a contract had been awarded to Birchwood Communications to install the cable system for a cost of $14,000. The equipment would be purchased from Cabletel Communications of Ontario for $75,000. Also, arrangements were being finalized with Island Telephone and Maritime Electric to use their poles to attach the cable. Claudette McNeill, manager of the Co-operative Council, said, 'It looks good that the system will be operating by Christmas' (R. Arsenault, 19 Nov. 1986).

At a meeting of the co-operative at the Evangeline regional high school during the first week of December, six directors were elected to guide the new enterprise. According to Gilles Painchaud, the new president, 'it was a bit of a nightmare at first.' He became involved when some of the original group came to him and requested that he stand for election. At first he was reluctant, but they explained that his knowledge of electronics and his technical skills would be crucial to the co-operative's success. As Gilles put it, 'I got involved when they made a co-op and they said we've got nobody to run it.' Active in many community causes and always ready for a challenge, he was a natural for the task of implementing the plans of the founding members.

The start-up of the service was not without its share of problems. The arrival of the equipment was delayed, so hook-ups did not begin until March of 1987. By then, commitments had been made that didn't make sense. For example, subscribers had been told that the co-operative would cover the costs of cable to their houses – even when they were as much as 1,000 feet from the road. Also the revenue of the co-operative was much less than projected because the estimates were based on 150–70 member-subscribers, but there were actually only 122. In addition, there were unforeseen supplementary costs. Maritime Electric and Island Telephone insisted that a large number of their poles must be replaced before they would allow the installation of the cable. At a charge to the cable co-operative of $400 per pole, this extra expense alone amounted to $15,000.

Consequently, on 10 June 1987, the board of directors held an emergency meeting to discuss the co-operative's financial problems. The president reported that although the budget submitted at the annual meeting the previous December projected a total cost of $99,000, the actual costs had come in at more than

$136,000. In order to deal with the financial shortfall, it was imperative to find additional members. The president, in describing the perilous financial situation, remained optimistic: 'We mustn't be discouraged. We must recruit new members.' At the same time he reaffirmed the co-operative's commitment to extend the cable system to the rest of the Evangeline region as soon as the first phase was on a sound financial footing. Supported by the majority of members present at the meeting, the co-operative decided to launch a recruitment campaign to add forty new subscribers in the first months of autumn (A. Cormier, 10 June 1987).

Reaching this objective required a good deal of effort. In Gilles Painchaud's words: 'We called people. We talked. We went around house to house.' As president, Gilles carried a particularly heavy load. Since the co-operative could not afford to pay a technician at $35 per hour, he did the work himself, in addition to his administrative duties. As he said years later, 'For the three years that I ran the organization as president, I would say that not a week went by that I didn't put in twenty hours of work on the co-operative's business.' The Co-operative Council also played a key role in the establishment of this cooperative. According to Darlene Arsenault, the council did everything from contracting the equipment companies, to ordering missing materials, to recruiting members and paying bills. Since the co-operative did not have its own staff, even the day-to-day administrative duties fell to the manager of the Co-operative Council.

Eventually the hard work paid off. Six months after the emergency meeting, membership in the co-operative had increased to 160. By the annual meeting on 31 May 1989, a little over one year later, it had increased to 185. This increase in subscriber-members ensured the financial viability of the co-operative. The 1989 balance sheet showed a net income before depreciation of the equipment of $13,244, with a slight deficit of $294 after depreciation. The co-operative had shown it could pay its way, but the revenue was not yet sufficient to undertake an expansion to the unserviced communities of Mont-Carmel and Cap-Egmont (R. Arsenault, 7 June 1989).

Early in 1990, Gilles, who worked for the Canadian Forces at

Summerside, was transferred to Halifax, and the co-operative elected another board of directors. Since the new directors did not involve themselves in the co-operative to the same extent as the previous board, the Co-operative Council (the second tier co-operative that acts as a co-ordinating body for the first tier co-operatives in Evangeline) was left to conduct the co-operative's day-to-day business. The manager of the Co-operative Council even found it difficult to get the board to agree to hold meetings to make necessary decisions. So while the co-operative's balance sheet continued to improve as the membership gradually increased, the strategic planning to achieve the co-operative's expansion objectives did not take place. The dreams of providing service to the whole region and of a community channel remained distant. Darlene expressed her disappointment about the slow progress: 'It's not going as fast as I would have liked it to go.'

In an effort to revitalize the cable co-operative, the Co-operative Council secured funding from the Department of Community and Cultural Affairs for a study that would identify expansion options. A local consultant was retained in November 1990, and a report was prepared. The consultant noted that the co-operative's membership had increased to 206, so that its financial situation was encouraging. Unfortunately the cost of cable had increased from $10,000 per mile to nearly $20,000, making the option of expanding the present system to sparsely settled areas too costly. He indicated that the installation of a VHF transmitter represented a second option, but experience in other areas showed uneven reception from such a system.

According to the consultant, a Multipoint Distribution System (MMDS) represented the best option. It would cost less than an extension of the existing cable system and would provide better reception than VHF. The consultant's proposal specified that the new MMDS system would be one component of a combination package that would also include a community channel, a community radio station, and a mini-studio for cable production and sound recording. The estimated cost of implementing these plans was $342,000. Of this amount, the consultant proposed that

$100,000 be raised locally, with the balance coming from the participation of both provincial and federal governments. The report recognized that governments do not as a rule fund cable systems. It was suggested, therefore, that this initiative might be viewed more favourably if it was presented as a strategy to preserve the French language and Acadian culture through the use of community communication tools (P.D.G. Consultants 1991).

The consultant's bold proposal galvanized the board of the cable co-operative into action. With the advice and assistance of the Co-operative Council, the cable co-operative set up an advisory committee chaired by Gilles Painchaud, the co-operative's first president, to review the report. Meanwhile, with the assistance of a grant from the federal Secretary of Francophone Affairs, the co-operative hired a staff person to search out funding possibilities. This initiative was pursued with vigour, but according to Claudette McNeill, 'Everywhere we applied, we didn't get anywhere.'

Without government funding, the proposal to combine an expansion of the cable service with the start-up of a community channel and the construction of a studio was no longer viable. The co-operative decided to proceed with an expansion on a scale that could be accomplished with its own resources. In April 1992, the Co-operative Council prepared a financial forecast for expansion that was used by the cable co-operative to negotiate an additional loan from the credit union. With financing in hand, the cable co-operative expected to apply to the CRTC for an expansion licence before the end of 1992.

THE PRINCE EDWARD ISLAND POTATO CHIP
CO-OPERATIVE

On the occasion of the official opening of the P.E.I. Potato Chip Co-operative, 25 March 1987, the president, Jean-Paul Arsenault, presented the first bag of Olde Barrel potato chips to Leonce Bernard, M.L.A. for the Evangeline region. Arsenault stated that he did so in recognition of Bernard's personal contribution to the project, as well as his support as a minister of the provincial government. Bernard responded that for him the opening of the co-operative was 'a dream come true.' He was enthusiastic about the project for two reasons: it was owned by the workers themselves; and it utilized the Island's potato resource to produce a value-added product. He added that 'if Islanders are as interested in the potato chips as they have been in the formation of the worker co-operative, the enterprise is bound to be successful.' In concluding the ceremony, Jean-Paul Arsenault informed those present that the campaign to launch Olde Barrel potato chips would include radio and television publicity across the Maritimes. The objective of the campaign would be to obtain, within three years, 10 per cent of the Maritime market for potato chips (R. Arsenault, 1 Apr. 1987).

According to Alcide Bernard, manager of the P.E.I. Potato Chip Co-operative, the Co-operative Council played an important role in the organization's origins. The main purpose of the Co-operative Council, which was founded in 1977, was to make sure that Evangeline people understood the philosophy of co-operatives. Although the Evangeline region had a number of successful co-operatives that had been formed in the 1930s, many younger people took them for granted. While some followed their parents' example of co-operative involvement, others saw no reason why they should participate in or even patronize the region's co-operatives. Reflecting upon the work of the Co-operative Council, Leonce Bernard described it as the means that was used 'to go back to that age group between twenty and forty that had lost the understanding of why co-operatives were formed ... to bring back to the population what we had lost.'

The Co-operative Council sponsored a series of small group meetings throughout the Evangeline region in the early 1980s to sensitize people to the potential of the co-operative movement in the region. At these 'kitchen meetings' participants talked about their desire to create additional employment opportunities for the region's youth. They specified, however, that they did not wish to do this by attracting outside firms to locate in the region. Instead they wanted to achieve their goal through the establishment of community-controlled enterprises.

At the same time, some of the members of the Co-operative Council were aware of the initiatives being taken in Quebec to promote the worker co-operative model as a means of creating community employment. Since they were interested in the possible application of the model to the Evangeline region, the manager of the Co-operative Council was instructed to investigate it. This information was shared and discussed at the small group meetings. In addition the meetings encouraged community members to voice their ideas and suggestions. Particular attention was paid to encouraging suggestions for employment generation that would both benefit farmers and create jobs in production enterprises. The idea of processing and manufacturing potato chips came up at one of these meetings.

The suggestion had surfaced for the first time a few years before as a proposal to the Baie Acadienne Industrial Commission. But the commission had dismissed it, thinking that it required too much capital. This time a number of influential people supported it, especially Leonce Bernard, member of the provincial legislature for the region. As chairperson of the Co-operative Council, he spearheaded local initiatives to make the idea a reality. Under his leadership, the Co-operative Council applied for and received funding from the provincial Department of Industry and the Baie Acadienne Venture Capital Group to send a study team from Evangeline to two potato-chip manufacturing firms in Philadelphia. On 18 November 1985, this team, consisting of three representatives from the Baie Acadienne Industrial Commission and the Baie Acadienne Venture Capital Group, accompanied Hal Parker, of the P.E.I. Department of Industry, on a visit to these manufacturing enterprises (R. Arsenault, 18 Dec. 1985). Upon their return, the study team made the information public at the first annual meeting of the Baie Acadienne Venture Capital Group, which had been organized by the Evangeline Credit Union to support the creation of community enterprises. At this meeting interested persons were invited to become part of an initiating group. Co-ordinated by the Co-operative Council, this group began to plan the development of the new co-operative. At their request the Baie Acadienne Industrial

Commission and the Evangeline Credit Union took responsibility for preparing a feasibility study and a business plan.

In early February 1986, this initiating group constituted itself formally as an interim board of directors of the new worker co-operative (R. Arsenault, 5 Feb. 1986). The board divided up the work by organizing committees in a number of functional areas: Land and Building, Finance, Personnel, and Rules and Regulations. As a necessary first step, the co-operative obtained agreements with local financial institutions (Evangeline Credit Union and Baie Acadienne Venture Capital Group) to invest $471,000. With local money committed, the co-operative negotiated with the provincial government for supplementary funding. These discussions were concluded successfully with the approval of a loan of $450,000 and a grant of $120,000 from the P.E.I. Development Agency ('Argents pour,' 16 Apr. 1986).

Informing the Community

One hundred and twenty-five people attended the co-operative's first public meeting to explain the project in early July 1986. Various aspects of the new worker co-operative were outlined, including the requirement that each worker-member must invest $5,400 in shares to help finance the operation. The initiators explained that the money could be borrowed from the Evangeline Credit Union and would be repaid by payroll deductions at the rate of $40 per week. It was also pointed out that the interim board of directors would continue to function until September 1987, by which time it was believed by the organizers that the employee-members would understand the functioning of the enterprise well enough to manage it themselves. They would then elect a board of directors from among themselves according to the principles of worker co-operatives. Since the Baie Acadienne Venture Capital Group and the Evangeline Credit Union had invested in the operation, their representatives would also attend board meetings in a non-voting capacity.

With respect to the jobs, there would be a manager, a director of marketing, a secretary, and two or three salespersons in the office. Ten people would be hired in the factory for such tasks as fork-lift operation, frying, product inspection, quality control, packaging, and shipping.

In terms of production, the president stated that the co-operative expected to make 400 pounds of chips a day from 1,600 pounds of potatoes. Three kinds of chips would be produced: regular, barbecue, and ripple. They would be cooked in cotton-seed oil, which would make the product lighter and less greasy than other chips. Salt would be the only preservative. The co-operative expected to obtain most of its potatoes from local producers, as long as producers could ensure a high-quality raw product.

The president painted an optimistic picture of expected sales. He told the assembly that although the co-operative would be in direct competition with large companies like Hostess and Humpty Dumpty, it hoped to obtain ten per cent of the Atlantic market within three years, for a total of $3.5 million dollars in annual sales. He thought this target would be achievable since it is likely that the potato chips would be sold under the co-operative label through Co-op Atlantic, the wholesaler for Atlantic region consumer co-operatives.

At the end of the meeting it was explained that hiring would begin in about two months. A selection committee would examine the qualifications of the applicants and would interview the best candidates. Persons who wished to be considered for employment could sign a list that evening to indicate their interest. To the surprise of the meetings' organizers, 110 persons signed the list, indicating that they were prepared to invest $5,400 of their own money (R. Arsenault, 6 Apr. 1986).

With funding in place and community interest ensured, preparations began to move more quickly. In July 1986, Wellington Construction, a local firm, was awarded the contract for the building at a cost of $270,000. The terms of the contract called for completion of the structure by the end of October. In July as well, the co-operative negotiated an agreement to purchase, for $400,000, the necessary production machinery from a firm in Harrisburg, Pennsylvania. This machinery was to arrive by the first of

November, so that production could begin before Christmas (R. Arsenault, 16 July 1986).

At this point, the selection of worker-members became a priority. Three people who had been part of the initiating group were the first staff hired – one as manager, and two for supervisory positions. Since someone was needed to co-ordinate the construction project, Alcide Bernard, as manager, started work immediately. Some fifty interviews were held for the remaining ten positions. While selection of the candidates was based on the skills required for a particular job, a candidate's record of participation in community organizations and other co-operatives was also part of the selection criteria.

With recruitment completed, the training of worker-members could be considered. One of the training priorities was for everyone involved to understand and become familiar with the worker co-operative model. To achieve this objective, the Co-operative Council arranged for personnel from the Desjardins Movement in Quebec to provide thirty hours of co-operative training. While the session was informative it may have been too short. One person reported, 'The training was too fast. I believe you'd need a couple of months training.' On the technical side, two supervisors were sent to the United States for one week to observe similar production lines in action. Training for the production-line workers took place on the job after production had begun. To facilitate this process the co-operative brought in a production expert from the United States to show worker-members how to use the equipment. This on-the-job training was also considered inadequate by some: 'We should have trained for six months. It should have been on the job elsewhere where there is somebody that knows what they're doing.'

In late August, the co-operative received unwelcome news that an additional $85,000 must be spent on an industrial waste system. Alcide was able to arrange for additional financing to cover these unexpected costs. The P.E.I. Development Agency agreed to purchase $70,000 in preferred shares, and the Evangeline Credit Union agreed to an additional $15,000 loan. However, more bad news was to come. Although the building was ready at the end of

October, the company producing the machinery informed the co-operative that the machinery shipment would be delayed until December. In fact this shipment didn't arrive until February 1987, so production could not begin until March (R. Arsenault, 10 Dec. 1986). Eric Arsenault, one of the worker-members, felt that this four-month delay had an adverse effect upon the new co-operative: 'We were supposed to have had the equipment in December ... and we didn't get the ball rolling until March. So there was a big negative factor right from the start.'

Production at the P.E.I. Potato Chip Co-operative officially began on 25 March 1987, four months after the projected start-up date. The delay had created difficulties for the worker-members. Since they had invested in December, they had to make payments on their loans although they were still unemployed. To make matters worse there were numerous production breakdowns. One machine in particular, which had been purchased second-hand, caused much of the problem. As a result the co-operative was not producing enough to break even on costs. For example, at the beginning workers produced only 108 cases of 12 bags in an eight-hour shift – roughly one-seventh of the 1992 rate of production. Even with low production levels, sales did not always keep pace. With a limited shelf-life, the product could not be produced too far in advance. This meant that worker-members were often employed on a part-time basis. One worker, Eric, lamented: 'We'd work one week and we'd have too much product. We couldn't sell it ... So we'd have to stop for a week.'

In spite of these early difficulties, both production and sales gradually improved. Customers liked the product and complimented the co-operative. One Charlottetown woman wrote that Olde Barrel potato chips were the best she had ever tasted. As proof, she stated that since their arrival she had doubled her consumption (R. Arsenault, 22 Apr. 1987). Although he did not provide any figures, Alcide Bernard reported in January 1988, less than a year after opening, that sales had exceeded expectations. He noted that most of the product had been sold through P.E.I. stores. The co-operative had originally contracted with Seaman's Beverages, the Pepsi-Cola distributor, to handle sales but had terminated the contract. The co-operative now employed its own salespersons and an increase in sales resulted. Sobey's, a large food-store chain on the Island, was an important customer. The co-operative had also hired two new salespersons for New Brunswick, which had also produced an increase in sales (R. Arsenault, 27 Jan. 1988).

While Sobey's, a private-sector firm, had been quick to pick up the new product, negotiations with Co-op Atlantic to sell Olde Barrel chips under the co-op label dragged on for a full year. Nevertheless, by June 1988, an agreement was finally concluded. This agreement was extremely important for it seemed to guarantee a minimum level of sales. However, the agreement did not live up to its promise. Just four months later, in October 1988, David Beals, food manager for Co-op Atlantic, announced that it was reducing purchases from the P.E.I. Potato Chip Co-operative. The reason cited by Beals was customer complaints about taste (J. Laforest, 2 Nov. 1988). According to members of the potato chip co-operative this was a total surprise. Since it happened without warning, the co-operative was unable to bring in people with expertise to rectify the problem. Nor did Co-op Atlantic offer to provide any assistance. One of the worker-members expressed his understanding of what happened this way: 'They just took the market from us. No warning or anything like that. Then we were in those one-half weeks again because we were producing too much for our market.'

Tom Webb, a spokesperson for Co-op Atlantic at that time, would neither confirm nor deny that the contract had been taken away without warning. He thought that the determination of who was to blame was less important than what could be learned from the termination of the contract. In retrospect, he would have liked Co-op Atlantic to have structured its involvement with the P.E.I. Potato Chip Co-operative in a more helpful way. In his view, the approach to co-operative development followed by Co-op Atlantic at that time could be thought of as a 'charity model.' Acting in good faith, but with little knowledge, Co-op Atlantic took a risk in granting the right to sell under the co-op label to a group of people with the best intentions, but with little experience and expertise.

He described this approach as 'all right and all wrong,' by which he meant that Co-op Atlantic's willingness to assist the P.E.I. Potato Chip Co-operative was all right, but the way it was done was all wrong. Co-op Atlantic underestimated the risk of its 'donation,' because it had not been a part of the development of the potato chip co-operative. Instead of the 'hands off' donor model, he preferred that Co-op Atlantic move to a stakeholder model of co-operation among co-operatives, which would emphasize mutual support and responsibility. Such a model of integrated co-operative development would mean that Co-op Atlantic as a stakeholder would play a major role in the development of new co-operatives. This role would involve not only the provision of business and technical expertise, but participation as well in the particular co-operative's decision-making structure.

While worker-members deplored what they considered Co-op Atlantic's precipitate action, they did not deny that they had difficulties maintaining the consistency of their product. They had started the enterprise without any experience in potato chip production. Although they had access by telephone to the expertise of their equipment supplier, to a large extent they had to learn on their own. One of the things they learned from bitter experience was the necessity to use only quality potatoes. Initially the co-operative bought from local growers who did not have the storage facilities to maintain their potatoes at a certain standard. Consequently the co-operative sometimes received raw product which varied from the specified criteria. This caused anomalies such as the clumping together of chips. Sometimes there were more dark chips than there should have been. As Eric Arsenault said, 'We didn't know enough about the raw product. It is the single most important thing ... If you don't have a good product coming in, you get a mediocre product coming out.'

In addition to losing its sales contract with Co-op Atlantic, the P.E.I. Potato Chip Co-operative now faced another dilemma. Although it had started with thirteen worker-members, by 1990 only seven remained. Of the six members who left, some went to jobs that offered a more reliable pay cheque. Others found the work too hard and left for health reasons. Whatever the reasons, the main concern for the co-operative was that these non-working members retained the right to vote. This anomaly stemmed from the lack of worker co-operative legislation in P.E.I. When the worker co-operative model was accepted, the only change made to co-operative legislation was to allow workers to be board members. Although the by-laws of the potato chip co-operative stated that only working members had the right to vote, they did not have the force of law. Consequently it was conceivable that non-working members could at some point take over the co-operative. The obvious solution to this problem was to reimburse the initial investment to non-working members. However, the co-operative's difficult financial situation made this impossible.

The concern about a take-over spilled over into the co-operative's recruitment of new members and access to new member investment. It had been intended that as additional full-time jobs became available, there would be opportunity for new members to join. A prospective member would purchase half the shares required for membership at the beginning of a six-month probation period. After probation, the member would buy the balance of the shares and be entitled to voting rights. But now this recruitment strategy was in question. According to the P.E.I. Department of Justice, a person must be granted full membership rights as soon as one share was purchased. This meant that all persons automatically became full members as soon as they started their probation period. As a result the potato chip co-operative did not recruit beyond the original seven worker-members. All other staff were hired workers. Alcide Bernard explained: 'It's too risky, so we haven't recruited anybody else since we found that out. It only takes one or two more now and the balance is outside.'

One consequence of this policy was that members began to accept it as normal. Some wondered whether they wanted to accept new members even if the legislation were changed. 'We've been through hard times. Why should we get new people now and they benefit?' Nevertheless, since the original purpose of the co-operative was to provide employment for the community, the board of directors decided to approve the recruitment of new members as soon as safeguards were built into the legislation.

After Co-op Atlantic withdrew its patronage, the potato chip co-operative was left on its own to find substitute markets. To achieve this goal, the co-operative embarked on a bold plan to set up its own sales distribution network throughout the Maritimes. Sixteen salespersons were hired, including a manager and supervisor. This was a costly move, but one that resulted in increased sales. In 1990-91 sales jumped to $3.4 million from $2.9 million one year earlier (J. Laforest, 5 Feb. 1992). Then suddenly the co-operative was faced with a new problem.

During the summer of 1991 the virus PVYN was found in the variety of potatoes used by the co-operative. Under pressure from potato growers from the United States, the P.E.I. government ordered the destruction of all potato crops suspected of the virus. Unable to obtain potatoes for production, the co-operative had no choice but to shut down for three weeks in June, and to stop their sales promotions since there was no product. When the co-operative finally obtained potatoes from the United States, it was at four times the local price. Once production resumed, salespersons reported a new customer resistance to P.E.I. potatoes. Apparently people were afraid of purchasing the chips for fear of catching the virus.

The recession also took its toll; people were buying less and looking for bargains. Even large companies like Hostess were reducing their prices. Commenting on the situation, Alcide Bernard said, 'Before this year, I have never seen chips sell at such a low price.' As well as paying a much higher than normal price for potatoes, the co-operative was also forced to lower prices to maintain existing sales levels. Considering all the obstacles, Alcide concluded that for co-operatives such as this to succeed there must be support mechanisms, with the capacity to provide specialized assistance in the areas of development, financing, and marketing (J. Laforest, 5 Feb. 1992).

The Current Situation

Unable to meet its operating requirements, the P.E.I. Potato Chip Co-operative went into receivership on 27 April 1992. After ten days without production, it was reopened under the trusteeship of Coopers and Lybrand (J. Laforest, 6 May 1992). Meanwhile discussions were being carried on, with the objective of saving the enterprise. These talks led to the restructuring of the co-op on 15 May, 1992, as the Island Potato Chip Co-operative. Shareholders in the new co-operative included Co-op Atlantic, the Evangeline Credit Union, and the Credit Union Central of P.E.I.

While Co-op Atlantic's name appeared on the document of incorporation, Ann Balch from that organization's member and public relations department made it clear that Co-op Atlantic had no intention of investing in Island Potato Chip Co-operative. Co-op Atlantic's role would be to provide expertise in the areas of financial planning and management control systems to ensure Island Potato Chip Co-operative's long-term viability. The role of the other signatories would be to furnish a line of credit during a transition period. John Martin of Co-op Atlantic's financial services division indicated that marketing problems may have played a key role in the P.E.I. Potato Chip Co-operative's failure. While he admitted that many co-operative stores had not been part of the Potato Chip Co-operative's distribution network, Martin indicated that Co-op Atlantic would feature Olde Barrel and ask its retail outlets to support the product. However, this arrangement did not endure and one year later the Island Potato Chip Co-operative was sold to an Ontario firm.

LA COOPÉRATIVE LES P'TITS ACADIENS

Les P'tits Acadiens, a women's worker co-operative that manufactured children's clothing, officially opened its doors on 15 October 1987. In addition to community members, the thirty-five well-wishers who attended the opening ceremony included the speaker of the P.E.I. legislature and the federal M.P. for the constituency. Representatives of the provincial Department of Industry and the federal Department of Employment and Immigration, both of which had assisted in the start-up of this co-operative, were also present. In her address, Colette Arsenault, the manager of Les P'tits Acadiens, pointed out that the new co-operative had two purposes: to produce good-quality children's clothing at a reasonable price, and to provide employment opportunities for the region. She said that the co-operative would employ five persons in the early stages, with the number increasing to ten within two years. In closing she thanked the various private and public agencies that had assisted in the organization of the project. Wilfred Arsenault, the second speaker, in his role as president of the provisional co-operative board, also thanked the various collaborators in the project. He especially praised the manager and the worker-members for the initiative they had shown in identifying the need for children's clothing and for creating an enterprise to meet that need. After a blessing by the priest, the ceremony concluded with a fashion show by local children, who modelled some of the outfits designed and produced in the co-operative's workshop (R. Arsenault, 21 Oct. 1987).

A Grassroots Idea

The idea of manufacturing children's clothing originated with Colette Arsenault, a young mother who was taking a year's leave of absence from teaching. For some time she had been dissatisfied with the quality, selection, and price of available children's clothing. One day after returning from shopping in Summerside, about a half hour's drive from Evangeline, she said to her husband, 'It's too bad we can't start a clothing manufacturing business.' He, a community leader and loans officer at the Evangeline Credit Union, responded by indicating that there were a number of government programs available to assist financially with such a project. After thinking about the idea for several days, Colette phoned Carmella Richard, a friend who had completed a clothing design course at Holland College in Summerside, to ask for her opinion. She also phoned three other women who she thought might be interested. Everyone agreed that the idea was a good one. After several meetings of the five women, they decided to proceed with the planning of a clothing production co-operative. Only Colette and Carmella were interested in employment for themselves.

On behalf of the group, Colette contacted both community and government institutions for assistance, for example, the provincially funded Evangeline Regional Services Centre and the St Thomas Aquinas Society. From this point onwards, Wilfred Arsenault, the economic development officer from the St Thomas Aquinas Society, became actively involved with the group. He attended all meetings and was particularly involved with the planning and organization of the project.

In a series of meetings in the women's homes, they planned how to proceed. Since two of the women wished to create employment for themselves rather than to provide a service to the community, the worker co-operative structure seemed the most appropriate. Wilfred Arsenault from the St Thomas Aquinas Society and Claudette McNeill from the Co-operative Council helped in discussions about starting and operating a worker co-operative. Wilfred drew up a business plan to guide the development process. Claudette assisted with the incorporation of Les P'tits Acadiens and with the setting up of the organization's by-laws.

The next area of concern for the group was training for worker-members. Only Carmella Richard had any knowledge of clothing production and none of the group had any experience running a business. A search for assistance identified only one person with knowledge of clothing production – a teacher of clothing design at Holland College in Summerside. When contacted by the group, she indicated that if financing for a training project could be arranged, she would be prepared to provide the instruction to Les P'tits Acadiens's members.

On 8 September 1986, Les P'tits Acadiens was incorporated as a worker co-operative, with a provisional board that included three community members and a representative from each of the St Thomas Aquinas Society and the Evangeline Co-operative Council. Soon after the board of directors began to discuss a training project with the Department of Employment and Immigration. Colette Arsenault recalled how the pace of development quickened at that time: 'The ball started going really too fast, and we weren't ready for anything. Like we should have waited but the programs were there and everything.' By Christmas, the new co-operative had received approval from the federal Department of Employment and Immigration for a work-training project that would provide fifty weeks of training allowances to the worker-members. The first fourteen weeks of the project would have an instructional focus, while the balance would consist of training on the job.

During this same period Les P'tits Acadiens requested and received assistance from the Baie Acadienne Venture Capital Group and the P.E.I. Development Corporation to conduct a feasibility study. This survey of local stores appeared to confirm the demand for good-quality children's clothing. In retrospect Colette realized that the study could not possibly have provided the co-operative with the market information necessary to proceed: 'They only checked a few stores ... We didn't have any samples at that point to go and show.'

At this time Les P'tits Acadiens also requested and obtained financial assistance from the provincial Department of Industry's Small Business Development Program and from the P.E.I. Development Corporation's Rent Incentive Program. The former provided 50 per cent of the capital cost of new equipment in the form of a forgivable loan of $15,000. The latter provided rent assistance starting at 100 per cent in the first year and declining to 40 per cent in the third year (R. Arsenault, 21 Jan. 1987). Though the financial assistance was welcome at the time, members of Les P'tits Acadiens now feel that it may have been more of a curse than a blessing. In order to obtain the loan, Les P'tits Acadiens was required by the funding agency to purchase new equipment, even though second-hand equipment was available at a much lower cost. A second condition imposed by the funder was that Les P'tits Acadiens had to operate out of a proper production facility, with all the start-up and overhead costs that this entailed, instead of beginning with a small home-based operation. Colette expressed her reservations this way: 'I felt we were forced to start big and we weren't ready. We didn't have the expertise.' In addition to the financial assistance received from government, Les P'tits Acadiens raised money locally. The Evangeline Credit Union loaned the project $15,000 and a further $5,000 was raised by the workers themselves through their investment in membership shares of $1,000 each.

On 19 January 1987, the training program commenced. The fourteen-week instructional program was divided into three parts. The first two weeks emphasized the roles and responsibilities of members of a worker co-operative, as well as the administration of the enterprise and the marketing of products. The Evangeline Co-operative Council assisted Holland College with this part of the training. The next six weeks consisted of a clothing production course at Holland College. The final six weeks, which took place in the co-operative's own workshop, consisted of learning production methods. Instruction for this final segment of the course was provided by a consultant from the Federal Business Development Bank (R. Arsenault, 29 Apr. 1987).

Looking back on this experience, the initiators of Les P'tits Acadiens agreed that the training program was inadequate. There was just too much to learn in such a short time. As Carmella Richard pointed out: 'The training was not good. It wasn't complete. They showed the members how to sew some clothing and basically that's all they were shown.' More specifically, co-operative members didn't learn enough about running a business. Colette Arsenault, the manager of Les P'tits Acadiens, stated, 'I hadn't had a lot of training in business management ... so there was a lot I didn't know.' She thought as well that the sessions on worker co-operatives did not prepare members for the dual role of worker and owner. This resulted in a lack of clarity about the role and authority of the manager that was never resolved to everyone's satisfaction. Colette states: 'There were some misunderstandings in the co-operative among the employees ... Even if you are a worker co-operative, the manager should be allowed to take certain decisions.'

As well, members of the Les P'tits Acadiens didn't learn enough about clothing production and pattern making. Colette pointed out that even during the short six weeks at Holland College, the trainees did not receive the full attention of the instructor, who had to continue to teach her regular classes. 'We were surplus to what the teacher was already teaching ... So she didn't have a lot of time to spend with us.'

In terms of production, the consultant from the Federal Business Development Bank, while familiar with large manufacturing plants in Montreal, had no experience with small-scale production. Wilfred Arsenault expressed his opinion this way: 'They were not shown anything about a production line ... But they got the production problems solved as time went by.'

Finally, the training program largely ignored the areas of purchasing and marketing. The minimal purchasing assistance that Les P'tits Acadiens received from the Federal Business Development Bank was less than helpful. During the training period, the consultant accompanied some of the members to Montreal to purchase the equipment and the clothing material, but the material turned out to be unsuitable. It could not be used and had to be sold at a loss.

Many of the problems that plagued Les P'tits Acadiens in its operational phase grew out of decisions that were taken before the co-operative had developed its clothing models and identified a market. Colette commented on the purchasing and marketing problems as follows: 'We bought material,' she lamented, 'which was a mistake because we hadn't marketed the clothes yet. We were going to make the clothes and then go out and market them.' For Wilfred this was 'going about it ass backwards.' Lacking knowledge and experience in all these areas, members of Les P'tits Acadiens had difficulty charting their own direction. 'We were getting advice from a lot of people at that point in time,' Colette recalls. 'There were too many people involved.'

Operation of Les P'tits Acadiens

Les P'tits Acadiens began production of children's clothing on 19 April 1987. The first customer was a new children's store in Charlottetown that liked the co-operative's products and placed several orders. However, this retailer quickly ran into financial difficulties, which resulted in bankruptcy. Not only did Les P'tits Acadiens not receive payment for clothes that had been sold, but for a long period of time was unable to obtain the unsold stock. When that clothing was finally returned, it was off-season and had to be sold below cost. After only six months of operation the co-operative required additional investment capital.

As part of a restructuring plan, Les P'tits Acadiens obtained an agreement from the P.E.I. Development Corporation to invest $25,000, contingent upon the co-operative raising a matching amount. The Les P'tits Acadiens then approached the Evangeline Credit Union for a business loan. The credit union refused the loan application, insisting instead upon personal loans to Les P'tits Acadiens' members. However, when members applied for personal loans, they were informed by the credit union manager that their husbands must act as co-signers. Colette recalled her annoyance with the manager's request: 'We refused. We said we were all working and we could take care of $5,000 each. So they finally accepted that. We never had a good working relationship with the credit union. They weren't there to give us advice.'

The financial restructuring of Les P'tits Acadiens was success-fully completed, but it had come at a price. Two of the original members left, preferring not to invest further in the co-operative, and were replaced by two other women from the community. In spite of the financial restructuring, the marketing of the clothing continued to pose serious problems. Les P'tits Acadiens had not received the assistance that it had hoped for from Co-op Atlantic, the second tier co-operative that serves consumer co-operatives in the Atlantic region. On one occasion Les P'tits Acadiens sent clothing samples to be shown at a Co-op Atlantic trade show in Moncton. To her dismay, Colette later discovered that the sam-ples had not been displayed. In desperation, she, with the assis-tance of a marketing consultant from the P.E.I. Development Corporation, went on a promotional blitz to the big co-operative stores in Nova Scotia and New Brunswick. This approach worked to some extent. Les P'tits Acadiens began to receive orders, but not for long. As wholesaler to Atlantic region co-operative stores, Co-op Atlantic objected to suppliers like Les P'tits Acadiens selling directly to the co-operative stores. Consequently the stores were discouraged from purchasing directly from Les P'tits Acadiens.

During this first year, Les P'tits Acadiens explored many avenues as it tried to find markets. One of these was to contract with a consultant from the Federal Business Development Bank to advise the co-operative on how to proceed. Although his three reports cost Les P'tits Acadiens several thousand dollars, Colette indicated that 'there was no concrete advice. It was just like philosophy on paper.' Another consultant, through the assistance of the P.E.I. Development Corporation, was asked to design specific articles for an Anne of Green Gables clothing line the co-operative was considering. Not only did the consultant's designs not look like the popular television depiction of Anne of Green Gables, but the proportions also were wrong. Apparently the consultant was familiar with designing adult clothing, but knew little about children's designs. To adjust the designs, members of Les P'tits Acadiens contacted their former instructor at Holland College for assistance.

In addition to the difficulties in locating a potential market, Les P'tits Acadiens was having trouble keeping prices at a competitive level. While their products were gaining recognition for their excellent quality, the extra care taken in production reduced the amount of output. Also the cost of overhead was too high. Starting without experience, with minimal knowledge of clothing manufacturing and a serious lack of capital, the co-operative found it difficult to get production up fast enough to compete with large manufacturing companies.

Knowing what advice to take and what to refuse had also been a problem during the first year. Since the members of Les P'tits Acadiens had little experience themselves, they tended to rely upon persons who were supposed to be experts. As this advice often proved to be unsatisfactory, Les P'tits Acadiens gradually learned that it must make its own decisions. Summarizing this experience Colette said: 'It took us almost a year to realize that we had to take things in our own hands and stop listening to everybody. But that was the year we lost a whole lot of money.'

As Les P'tits Acadiens had experienced so much difficulty breaking into the market for children's clothing, the co-operative decided in the second year to switch to the production of gym clothes, such as fleecewear sweatshirts and nylon pants for both children and adults. With the prospect of the Canada Winter Games and the Acadian Games coming to P.E.I., there seemed to be a ready-made market. Samples and sales contacts were made. This change in direction was a positive one, which allowed Les P'tits Acadiens to continue to remain in business.

Subsequently, Les P'tits Acadiens concentrated on breaking into the school and college market. It was tough sledding at first, but by the end of the second year, when Colette, pregnant with her third child, left Les P'tits Acadiens, sales had increased significantly. With Carmella Richard in charge, Les P'tits Acadiens continued production for another two years. Through developing contacts with the schools of P.E.I., the co-operative seemed to have found a market niche. Carmella reported that 'the first two years, we really had to dig for orders. But afterwards, it seemed that people would phone us whenever there was an activity and would want to order sweats from us.' The reason for this sales turnaround seems to have been that as a small producer Les P'tits Acadiens could tailor production to the customers' needs. In Carmella's words: 'They could order twelve sweatshirts, of different sizes and different colours, which you can't do when you place an order with a large manufacturer. So we were filling those little potholes.'

Still, maintaining Les P'tits Acadiens was an ongoing struggle. Because there were not enough orders to keep the co-operative going year-round, overhead costs piled up during the three or four months of non-production. Members were only able to pay themselves slightly above minimum wage, and during periods of non-production they sometimes had to work without wages.

After four years of production, the members decided to shut down their business. When the equipment was sold and the bills paid, Les P'tits Acadiens was able to return to members $1,200 of their original investment of $6,000. Ironically, the last year of Les P'tits Acadiens' operation had been its most successful, with sales finally reaching the first year's target of $100,000. And there had been no need to look for orders; they just kept coming in. In the end, however, non-business factors precipitated the decision. The manager, Carmella Richard, decided to leave Les P'tits Acadiens since she was expecting twins and wanted to be at home with them. The other three members were uncertain whether they wished to continue without her. At this juncture, while the members were trying to decide what to do, a new clothing design co-operative starting up in Charlottetown offered to purchase their equipment. This offer tipped the balance, and Les P'tits Acadiens closed in June 1991 (J. Laforest, 13 Feb. 1991).

According to Wilfred Arsenault, the closure was understandable. From his perspective, the co-operative had faced almost insuperable obstacles in the areas of production, marketing, business management, and financing. The members had learned much on the job, as they struggled to overcome these barriers. However, the gradual improvement had come at the price of a loss of enthusiasm to continue. Arsenault states, 'You know, you get tired of it, so you pack it in, right! No one got screwed. No supplier didn't get paid. They were not forced to close. They decided to pack up and quit.'

While Les P'tits Acadiens was unable to sustain itself, the initiators felt that they had learned a great deal from the project. Wilfred described it as 'a learning experience for me and I think for the community.' As a facilitator of community efforts, he would adopt a more cautious approach in the future. He would take much greater care to ensure that an initiating group had within it the expertise that a particular project required. He would also be more concerned that such a project had adequate financial backing.

Colette reported that if she had the chance to start again, she would do things very differently. One of the changes she would make would be to rely less upon so-called experts. Instead of dealing with a large number of consultants from a variety of agencies, she would prefer to deal with one or two, who would be involved with the project on an ongoing basis. She would not accept consultants' advice so readily, but would rely more on her own common sense: 'Now if people start giving me advice, I am more able to pick and choose.'

A second change would be to proceed with the project more slowly and deliberately so as to make sure that every alternative and its consequences were considered. 'We didn't consider whether to go with piece-work or to go into a manufacturing business ... I would never start in a year.' A third change would be to give marketing and training a much higher priority. She would not want to make production decisions in advance of the establishment of markets. She would try to ensure that the training was relevant to the actual manufacturing tasks to be performed.

A final change, perhaps most significant of all, would be to place less emphasis on obtaining government grants. She now recognizes that acceptance of the grants imposed certain conditions upon Les P'tits Acadiens. To satisfy the funding requirements, the co-operative had been forced to operate according to a full-time employment, industrial production model. Yet both her own and Carmella's difficulties in combining the roles of worker and mother demonstrated that this model was not appropriate for many Evangeline region women. According to Colette the grants actually decreased Les P'tits Acadiens' chances of success by establishing inappropriate requirements: 'I think if the government hadn't been involved and we could have bought the equipment second-hand and gone for piece-work from home, we would probably have been able to swing it.'

In assessing their involvement with Les P'tits Acadiens, members have emphasized the learning experience for themselves and for the community. Les P'tits Acadiens also had a positive economic impact upon members and the community, even though it was not ultimately sustainable as a business enterprise. While it is true that members lost most of their original investment, they gained other benefits, including transferable skills. Currently two of the women are employed part-time as seamstresses, working out of their homes. Others plan to use what they learned to start their own businesses.

Conclusion

The narratives of the four case studies describe the process through which the four co-operatives under consideration were formed. These narratives provide a foundation for further analysis, a task to which we now turn.

3
Interpreting the Case Histories

This chapter examines how the factors associated with the formation of the four case studies discussed in chapter 2 have operated to support or limit the co-operatives' formation and development. Six factors have been identified: (1) the attitudes, perspectives, and actions of initiators and members of organizing committees; (2) the response of community members and organizations to initiators' actions; (3) the contributions of institutional leaders; (4) the contributions and limitations of community development organizations; (5) the role of external agencies and organizations; and (6) the manner of project preparation.

1. ATTITUDES, PERSPECTIVES, AND ACTIONS OF INITIATORS AND MEMBERS OF ORGANIZING COMMITTEES

Sense of attachment to, and identification with, fellow community members served as the primary motivators for the initiators' involvement in the formation of the four co-operatives. Feelings of attachment to the community also contributed to the confidence that initiators and members of organizing committees exhibited. Their feeling of connectedness to their community allowed them to trust that their efforts to form co-operative organizations would receive a supportive response. They demonstrated this confidence through the ease with which they shared their ideas with others and the comfort they demonstrated in enlisting the involvement of community members and leaders.

Feelings of attachment to the Evangeline region and its people also provided the basis for a movement perspective rooted in an awareness of the distinctive needs and aspirations of Acadian people. This perspective took into account the well-being of the whole community, and valued social and cultural needs equally with economic ones. This perspective also included the notion of self-reliance through community control as the means for the Evangeline region to maintain its distinctive viewpoint and way of life.

Especially in the formation of the two community service co-operatives (Chez Nous and the Community Communications Co-operative), feelings of attachment played an important part in motivating the involvement of the initiators and members of the organizing committee. Initiators connected themselves and their own welfare to that of the community. With Chez Nous, they identified strongly with the concerns of seniors. Amand Arsenault stated that 'our old people are part of us.' Lorraine Arsenault described how stories about the unhappiness of seniors who had been moved to a Summerside nursing home motivated her to act: 'If I can be instrumental in stopping the hurt and ache of somebody that has to move their old parents out of their old French home and put them in an English place ...' A number of other members of the organizing committee also explained their commitment to Chez Nous in terms of their identification with the needs of the region's seniors. Eric Arsenault understood their discomfort: 'The old people don't feel comfortable there [in Summerside]. They don't understand the doctors. So that's why there's a lot of interested people around here who want to build the building.' Ida Gallant felt their sadness: 'When people came there and spoke French, you could see her eyes, you know – and theirs too. So that's what motivated us to try and get something to keep them here.'

Persons involved in the formation of the cable co-operative explained their involvement primarily in terms of their cultural identification as French-speaking Acadians. They felt deeply that a cable system that broadcast only in English would destroy the community's capacity to maintain its French language and

Acadian culture. The St Thomas Aquinas Society's brief to the CRTC, which opposed the M1 Rural Television Cable System application, expressed this fear: 'The addition of seven English-language stations will be another blow to our already menaced French minority and to our young people who will face increasing pressures to assimilate' (R. Arsenault, 12 June 1985).

While initiators' attitudes of attachment to the community played a lesser role in the formation of the two worker co-operatives, Les P'tits Acadiens and the P.E.I. Potato Chip Co-operative, they were still an important contributing factor. In the case of Les P'tits Acadiens the planning group was composed not only of persons who wanted to create employment for themselves, but also of friends who wanted to help establish a new community business. Colette Arsenault stated that: 'community members who did not intend to find employment were willing to get involved.' With the potato chip co-operative, the planning group was composed not only of farmers who wished to sell their produce and persons who hoped to find employment, but also of supportive community members who had a vision of creating jobs for the Evangeline region.

Unlike the service co-operatives, however, where the dominant purpose of formation was the welfare of the community, the worker co-operatives had the dual purpose of providing benefit both to specific persons and to the community. For the initiators who became working members of these co-operatives, the dual objectives sometimes became a source of tension when attitudes of self-interest clashed with attitudes of attachment to community. Eric Arsenault alluded to this tension when he compared his personal view, that the P.E.I. Potato Chip Co-operative was formed to benefit the community, with that of other worker-members, who viewed it as their personal, collective enterprise: 'You don't think of yourself. You think of future generations. There is potential for receiving returns on your investment. But that's not the key issue ... Most of the people who invested in our co-operative had the concept of putting money in their pocket.'

Alcide Bernard pointed out that these conflicting attitudes have resulted in an ongoing debate among the members of the potato chip co-operative about whether to recruit new members or keep the business for themselves: 'There is a tendency to want to keep the business for themselves, so it is necessary to continually go back to co-operative principles.' In spite of this ongoing dilemma, the board of the co-operative has continued to support the co-operative principle of open membership, although the lack of appropriate co-operative legislation has limited the application of this support in practice.

A second feeling that lay behind the behaviour of the initiators and members of the organizing committee was that of confidence. They seemed to have a strong sense of agency that they could do something about their situation, and moreover they were willing to become involved in collective risk-taking to realize their aspirations. Eric Arsenault's reaction to being asked to join the co-operative exemplified this attitude: 'I've always been confident from day one, as soon as they asked me. It sounded interesting so I just had to jump in. I always had a good feeling about producing potato chips. There's no reason why it shouldn't work.' Leonce Bernard demonstrated a similar attitude in his support for a community cable system. 'If somebody else can do it, we can do it too.' Lorraine Arsenault showed this same determination toward the community-care centre: 'We weren't going to quit now, especially when the residents were asking us when we're going to get it done.'

The source of this confidence can be traced back to the linkages of the initiators with the people of their community and the expectation that they would receive community support for their efforts. Lorraine expressed a profound sense of trust that the community would get behind Chez Nous: 'Because anything you start, they always jump in with you.' In struggling to understand what kept her working on the cable co-operative when the obstacles to achieving it seemed so great, Darlene Arsenault concluded that it was the feeling that she wasn't alone. The cable co-operative would have been too much to achieve alone, but by working in a partnership with others, anything felt possible: 'There's certain things that you can't do by yourself. It's impossible. And you don't get the motivation by yourself, compared to working with a group. Sometimes I thought that the community cable was ridiculous. We'll never get past it. It's too much money. It's too much that. And the people would say, "Yes we can do it. We can!"' For Gilles Painchaud, an outsider, who is now a permanent resident in the Evangeline region, the extraordinary sense of agency that he has observed derives from the propensity of people to collaborate with one another. 'When people get an idea, their first impulse is to get together to see what they can do.'

The initiators and organizers of these co-operatives viewed themselves as part of a collectivity of the Acadian nation with an awareness of the distinctiveness of their language, culture, and co-operative institutions. To this awareness was added the desire to maintain their particular way of life. Whereas the dominant culture stresses individualism and the separation of the economic from the cultural and social, the Acadian way emphasizes interdependence and the integration of social, cultural, and economic concerns. From this perspective, the well-being of the community and all its members takes precedence over that of any particular group. The community's social and cultural well-being is regarded as inseparable from its economic well-being.

Concern for the welfare of the whole community was the dominant perspective in the four case studies. Lorraine Arsenault described how the initiators of Chez Nous changed their mind about setting up a worker co-operative when they realized that this model might limit community support. First and foremost, their purpose was to make the service available to all community residents: 'It's not to make money to give rebates to the workers. The money is just to be able to look after those people and pay the people that would be working there.' Amand Arsenault commented that the most difficult task was not the construction project itself, but keeping the price low enough so that all seniors, many of whom had only their old age pensions, could afford it. 'We want something that's affordable,' he stated bluntly.

A primary concern of the cable planning group was that all of the region have access to service. Darlene Arsenault, one of the organizers, argued: 'We thought our community is not just

Abram-Village and Wellington. We had Cap-Egmont and Mont-Carmel, and there was no talk of expansion or anything.' Echoing Darlene's concerns, Leonce Bernard stated that 'if there's money to be made we can reinvest that in the community to offer service beyond.' Finally, the initiators of the P.E.I. Potato Chip Co-operative and Les P'tits Acadiens emphasized that their purpose was to create jobs for the whole region. Colette Arsenault explained it this way: 'Our dreams at that time were to break even, to be able to operate year round, and to create jobs.'

In addition to valuing the needs of all members of the community, initiators of the Evangeline co-operatives had an integrative view of development. They understood that because social, cultural, and economic needs are not divisible, genuine development must take all of these needs into account. Consequently, even though job creation was a priority for the region, they did not subordinate their efforts to this end. The cable co-operative was considered worthwhile because it sought to preserve the culture. Chez Nous was considered worthwhile because it would provide a necessary service. The five to eight jobs that Chez Nous would create were considered a side benefit.

In forming these four co-operatives, the initiators emphasized self-reliance, as reflected in control by the community, and thereby rejected arrangements that would introduce external control over any aspect of Evangeline community life, whether social, cultural, or economic. In forming the cable co-operative, Darlene Arsenault was concerned that the provision of cable by M1 Rural would harm French-language usage and end the dream of having a community channel: 'We would never get it. It was a real brick wall.' Eric Arsenault opposed the idea of an external owner of the potato chip plant on economic grounds: 'They'd have the profits in their pocket. I'm sure they wouldn't come back to the community.' Amand Arsenault's opposition to the entrepreneur who wanted to build a community-care facility was also based on economic grounds since there would be no guarantee that local people would be hired: 'We don't want anybody controlling our lives.' Louise Arsenault opposed having the nursing-care facility owned by an outsider because it would reduce community involvement. 'We wouldn't be working together. We'd be working for this guy here.' For Ida Gallant the advantage of community control was to keep the cost low for the senior citizens. 'We want the control. That's why we didn't want an outsider to come in. We wanted a co-operative so we can set the price according to what it's going to cost.' Finally, for Eric Arsenault the importance of a self-reliant strategy was to keep the community economically viable, 'to keep money in your community and to keep our people together.' For Alcide Bernard, community control of the economy through co-operatives was crucial to the maintenance of the Evangeline region's cultural strength and vitality: 'People don't realize that co-operatives are keeping the community together. Having the co-operatives is a way to maintain the culture in this area.'

The ideas for all four co-operatives came directly from members of the Evangeline community, and more so from their life experiences. With respect to Chez Nous, the cable co-operative, and the potato chip co-operative, concern for community needs provided the motivating forces – the happiness of the seniors, the preservation of the French language, and the creation of employment opportunities. Lorraine described how the idea for Chez Nous came to her and Louise: 'We were going by a school that was for sale and she said to me, "Why don't we buy that and fix it up and take in these old people ...?" And I said, "You know, that's an idea. Let's try it just for fun."' With Les P'tits Acadiens, the motivating concern was a more private one – access to durable and moderately priced children's clothing. Even in this case, however, initiators thought in terms of the need for children's clothing in the community, as well as the potential for community employment opportunities. Colette Arsenault described the starting-point: 'I just said to my husband, "It's too bad we can't start a clothing manufacturing business." And he said, "The money's there."'

With respect to three of the co-operatives (Chez Nous, the Community Communications Co-operative, and Les P'tits Acadiens), the persons who experienced the concern initiated the action. The initiators of Chez Nous went to the Evangeline Credit

Union to find out the price of the vacant school that was for sale. As well, they sought out two community leaders to obtain information about how to proceed. The person who first learned of M1 Rural's plans for cable television sought help from the manager of the Co-operative Council to inform community leaders and obtain their views. The initiator of Les P'tits Acadiens phoned her friends to see what they thought of the idea, and after that she approached the St Thomas Aquinas' economic development officer for assistance. In all three cases, the initiators' actions resulted in the formation of organizing committees to develop the ideas and to formulate and implement plans for their realization.

The formation of the organizing committee for the P.E.I. Potato Chip Co-operative took place somewhat differently. It resulted from the planned intervention of an institutional structure rather than the voluntary actions of individuals. The Co-operative Council, acting as a community development organization, initiated a series of 'kitchen meetings' to involve Evangeline region residents in a process of reflection on community needs and possibilities. Among the ideas put forward was that of a potato chip plant. In this situation the individual who initiated the idea did not carry it forward. The idea was picked up enthusiastically by Leonce Bernard, a prominent community leader who was at that time president of the Co-operative Council. Under his leadership, the Co-operative Council became involved in a search for information to determine the project's feasibility, and a planning group of more than twenty people was put in place to direct the project. In that case, the Co-operative Council rather than an individual became the initiator of action.

2. THE RESPONSE OF COMMUNITY MEMBERS AND ORGANIZATIONS TO INITIATORS' ACTIONS

The positive response of community members and organizations to the actions of initiators and members of organizing committees has contributed significantly to the formation and development of the four co-operatives. Not only has the expectation of a positive community response provided the initiators of the co-operatives with the confidence to act on their ideas, but community support has made the implementation of these ideas possible. According to Lorraine Arsenault, community support was the most important factor in making the dream of a community-care centre a reality: 'I'd say community and the people's backing were the most important. We wouldn't have got anywhere without the people's backing.' This was true for Ida Gallant as well. 'We got 100 per cent support from the community.' For Darlene Arsenault, community support, defined as the willingness of people to work together to satisfy common needs, meant that together the community was able to accomplish what would have been impossible for anyone alone: 'So we were pulling together. We were working on it together. We weren't working on it by ourselves. Because I think that by oneself it would have been too big.' Community organizations and community members provided support in at least three ways: co-operation and financial contributions; willingness to volunteer for committee work; and participation in meetings and special events.

The extent of co-operation between community organizations and their financial contributions to the four co-operatives was impressive. During the organization of the Community Communications Co-operative, nineteen community organizations responded to the Co-operative Council's request for briefs supporting the community's cable application. With the P.E.I. Potato Chip Co-operative, all the community development organizations worked together to assemble funding and prepare for the start-up. For Chez Nous more than a dozen organizations – parishes, municipalities, social clubs, and private businesses – sponsored activities to raise funds for the proposed community-care facility.

Those organizations that did not sponsor activities made cash donations. Many of these donations were relatively large, with the funeral co-operative donating $22,000, the co-op store $1,000, the credit union $5,000, the Legion $10,000 over five years, and the Legion Auxiliary $6,000 over the same period. A large number of community members also contributed generously to Chez Nous. While many contributed cash, others made in-kind contributions, which ranged from the donation of quilts, wall hangings, and a quarter of beef, to the promise of hours of labour at the construction site, and donation of the land for the building.

Financial contributions to the Community Communications Co-operative took place through the purchase of $50 membership shares. Initially the number of shares sold was disappointing, but after the initiators made house-to-house visits to explain the importance of a membership purchase, the number dramatically increased from 122 to 160 and eventually to 185. Unlike the two service co-operatives, the worker co-operatives did not receive financial support from either community members or community organizations. For them, community financial support came solely from their worker-members and from the specialized community development organizations (for example, the Baie Acadienne Venture Capital Group and the Evangeline Credit Union).

The encouragement and volunteer commitments that initiators received were additional forms of community support. For all four co-operatives the experience of initiators sharing their ideas with community members and leaders was a positive one, which resulted in offers to help. Community leaders responded enthusiastically to the idea of a community-care centre: 'Now you've really got an idea,' said Amand Arsenault. When the initiators of Chez Nous asked community members to serve on a planning committee, all seventeen persons approached agreed to make the commitment. Similarly, with the other co-operatives, there was no difficulty finding volunteers to work on the projects. According to Leonce Bernard, volunteering to support such community projects comes about because people feel part of the community and therefore are prepared to give their time to accomplish something they view as important: 'When you are involved in the community and you believe in something and people ask you to serve on somewhere, it's awful hard to say no.'

The attendance of the general public at meetings and special events was also a form of support. Some sixty people came to a public meeting arranged by Chez Nous to explain the initiators' ideas, while more than 125 people attended an informational meeting sponsored by the P.E.I. Potato Chip Co-operative. Involvement of the community through special events was also a hallmark of the organizing process of Chez Nous. Starting with a rocking chair 'rockathon' which raised $8,000, the community participated in bingos, dances, pot-luck suppers, and musical concerts, events that were attended by as many as five hundred people.

3. THE CONTRIBUTIONS OF INSTITUTIONAL LEADERS

In the Evangeline region, federal and provincial government services are provided through the Regional Services Centre, which is located in the village of Wellington. It houses, as well, all of the region's voluntary and cultural agencies, most of which receive government funding. In sharp contrast to most rural areas, where professional and managerial positions are often held by outsiders and are located in urban centres outside the region, all government employees and all employees of cultural and voluntary agencies located in the Regional Services Centre are at the same time members of the Evangeline region communities. This unusual situation, in which essentially all of the government-funded leadership positions in the community are held by community members, can be explained by a 1988 agreement between the federal and provincial governments on the promotion of official languages. According to this agreement government services must be delivered in both official languages. The agreement effectively guarantees that Evangeline community members will obtain the region's government-funded jobs. Amand Arsenault explained the situation this way: 'Over here we're all from the community and that's because of the language issue. They are all bilingual positions and those bilingual positions come mainly from residents of the area here.'

Similarly, in the co-operative sector, the management positions (with the exception of the Mont-Carmel Co-operative Association, and the Acadian Co-operative Fishermen's Association, whose manager comes from Tignish) are held by community members. Many of these managers have obtained advanced education outside Prince Edward Island and have returned to the Evangeline region bringing specialized skills. Since Evangeline region citizens provide themselves with most of their services through their system of co-operatives, the managers of these co-operatives are a major leadership resource in the community.

The impact of having a significant number of community members in paid leadership positions, where they are able to devote some of their time and expertise to community issues, has been extremely important. While the ideas for the four co-operatives came from the life experiences of community members, it was their partnership with institutional leaders that allowed the the co-operatives to overcome the roadblocks and to bring their ideas to fruition. Eight of the twenty-three persons involved in the original organizing committees of the four co-operatives occupied paid leadership positions in the community. In addition three of these leaders were involved in the formation of more than one of the four co-operatives.

There are a variety of reasons why institutional leaders who are also community members are likely to play a more effective role in the development of co-operatives than outsiders who come and go. The initiators of the co-operatives knew and trusted them, and therefore found it easy to approach them with their ideas. Also the institutional leaders did not view their work in the community as just a job. Since they were working with friends and neighbours in their own community, the job was connected to their personal life. Thus their commitment was not only professional but personal as well.

Amand Arsenault indicated his understanding of the tension between his role as a government employee involved in community development and his position as a community member, but stressed the priority of his commitment to the community: 'I do have a responsibility to government. You have to keep your limitations in mind as a community resource person. But I would find myself a community person first. Because if they had offered me a job in Charlottetown, I would have refused.' Ida Gallant, one of the initiators of Chez Nous with whom Amand worked closely, expressed her understanding of Amand's commitment to the community when she said, 'Because of where we worked, even if it's for the government, it's for the community.'

Having local people fill paid leadership positions in the community not only made these positions (and the institutions they represented) more accountable, but also provided opportunities for leadership development. These positions helped retain talented young people in the community, encouraged others to return, and additionally offered opportunities for local people to develop their knowledge and skills. Through their linkage with their counterparts in external organizations, community leaders had the chance to expand their horizons and to become aware of other possibilities.

An example of this phenomenon was the decision by Leonce Bernard, then manager of the Evangeline Credit Union, to obtain the approval of his board of directors to set up the Baie Acadienne Venture Capital Group, after being exposed to information about the Spanish Mondragon co-operatives. Having access to the paid leadership positions in the region also provided community members with legitimization and material incentives to take action on behalf of the community. This is illustrated by Darlene Arsenault's comment that she probably wouldn't have taken the initiative to organize against M1 Rural if she hadn't been employed as a community agent for the St Thomas Aquinas Society: 'I probably wouldn't have done it, unless somebody had approached me and asked me what I thought of it and what we should do. If somebody had asked me to sit on the committee, I would probably have said yes. But if they hadn't, I wouldn't have volunteered. Because we are involved enough. I mean there's maybe 150 different committees in a population of 2,500. So that means you could go to meetings nearly every night.' Institutional community leaders have played such roles as animator, researcher, technical expert, and co-ordinator in the formation of the four co-operatives. As animators, institutional community leaders were particularly important in the formation of the cable co-operative and the potato chip co-operative. With respect to the cable co-operative, Darlene Arsenault, through her work as a community agent, became aware of the M1 Rural Television and

Cable Systems' plan to obtain the cable licence. Appalled by the news, she shared the information with leaders of Evangeline region community organizations. This led to the organization of a group to oppose the application, and ultimately to the creation of the Community Communications Co-operative. In terms of the potato chip co-operative, the idea was generated at a community meeting where it might have died had not Leonce Bernard taken the initiative. This led to the involvement of community and government institutions to provide funding to assess the feasibility of producing potato chips, and the formation of an organizing committee.

Although Leonce was an important animator for the potato chip co-operative, he had played a similar role for other projects as well. While manager of the Evangeline Credit Union in the late 1970s, he had spearheaded the formation of two key development organizations to provide support to new projects. These were the Baie Acadienne Venture Capital Group, which had the capacity to provide grants and equity investments to new enterprises, and the Co-operative Council, which among other functions, played an animating role to involve the community in an ongoing self-development process.

A second role played by institutional leaders, particularly in the important area of assistance with funding, was that of researcher and resource person. Institutional leaders, through their respective organizations, were in a position to research the facts needed for feasibility studies and business plans. Thus, Amand Arsenault obtained information about worker co-operatives to help the P.E.I. Potato Chip Co-operative, and Claudette McNeill and Wilfred Arsenault obtained cost estimates for the Community Communications Co-operative and Les P'tits Acadiens respectively. Information about resources and the ability to access them was also necessary. Amand was able to obtain a community planner from the Department of Community and Cultural Affairs to prepare a preliminary sketch for the community-care facility as well as funding for Chez Nous to hire its own co-ordinator. Wilfred accessed training funds from Employment and Immigration Canada for Les P'tits Acadiens. Alcide Bernard, with assistance from Leonce, obtained grants and loans from the P.E.I. Development Corporation.

Institutional leaders provided technical advice to the co-operatives in such areas as business planning and incorporation. However, they lacked the specialized knowledge required by co-operatives that produced goods for export beyond the region. With Les P'tits Acadiens, there was a lack of local knowledge of the intricacies of clothing production processes, design, and marketing, and as a result the project became too dependent upon outside consultants and advisers, who often had little accountability or commitment to the co-operative. With the P.E.I. Potato Chip Co-operative there was a lack of manufacturing and marketing expertise. As a result the co-operative had to learn a great deal by trial and error, which had a negative effect upon sales and eventually upon the co-operative's financial viability.

Institutional leaders often provided the co-operatives with ongoing developmental assistance. Since four of the seven members of both the Community Communications Co-operative and the P.E.I. Potato Chip Co-operative were institutional leaders, this role was shared to a greater extent than in the formation of the other two co-operatives. However, Amand Arsenault and Claudette McNeill, as managers of the Evangeline Co-operative Council, provided some co-ordinating functions through arranging the meetings of the organizing committees. With Les P'tits Acadiens and Chez Nous respectively, Wilfred and Amand Arsenault played this developmental role. Both attended all group meetings to assist with planning and problem-solving. Wilfred describes his involvement as follows: 'I attended all the work meetings. I helped with every aspect of putting things together.' Amand saw his role as making sure that the group had the information it needed to make decisions, and in assisting the group to become increasingly competent to deal with the issues before it: 'With the level of expertise that we had on the original committee, we had to bring it along at a very slow pace to make sure each step was clear before moving on to the next stage.'

4. EVANGELINE REGION COMMUNITY DEVELOPMENT
ORGANIZATIONS

Institutional support for the development of the four co-operatives has come from five community development organizations:
The Evangeline Co-operative Council, the Evangeline Credit
Union, the Baie Acadienne Venture Capital Group, the Baie Acadienne Industrial Commission, and the St Thomas Aquinas Society. The Evangeline Co-operative Council, an umbrella organization representing the region's co-operatives, was set up in 1977
to stimulate and co-ordinate co-operative development in the
region. During the mid-1980s the Co-operative Council began to
focus its energies upon economic development. In 1985, the Evangeline Credit Union set up a subsidiary, the Baie Acadienne Venture Capital Group, to supplement its own capacity to make risk
capital available to co-operatives and private community business. Equity of the Baie Acadienne Venture Capital Group came
from forgone patronage dividends of members of the Evangeline
Credit Union, topped up by federal and provincial tax credits.

The Baie Acadienne Industrial Commission is a quasi-govern-
ment body set up under the P.E.I. Department of Industry to promote economic development. In the Evangeline region, the
Industrial Commission is directed by a six-member local board
representing the parish of Mont-Carmel and the municipalities of
Wellington and Abram-Village. Although funded by the Department of Industry, the Industrial Commission has the responsibility for hiring its own staff person and setting its priorities based
on local needs. The St Thomas Aquinas Society, a cultural organization dedicated to the survival of the French language and Acadian institutions, has historically concerned itself with both
economic and cultural development.

Community development organizations, in conjunction with
community leaders, have to some extent institutionalized the formation and development of co-operatives in the Evangeline
region. These established social institutions with a foundation
that is both organizational and financial have been able to provide continuity to the development process. While not replacing

the voluntary initiatives of individuals and groups, the development organizations have galvanized and supported members of the community in many projects.

According to Leonce Bernard such support is critical to the formation of co-operatives. Because co-operatives have to gather people and resources together, people must be deliberately encouraged to work collectively. Even though the Evangeline region had a history of solidarity and of co-operation, community leaders found it necessary to form the Co-operative Council to re-invigorate the tradition. As pointed out by Leonce, one of its first initiatives was to sponsor small-group meetings that brought community members together to reflect upon how they had met their needs in the past through co-operatives, and to consider what might be done in the future: 'The Co-operative Council undertook a process of motivation of the population that was very successful. The main principle of the Co-operative Council from 1977 was exactly to bring back to the people what we had lost, because when the co-operatives were formed in the thirties, it was not by magic. They were formed because there was a need.' As has already been pointed out, this process led to the formation of the potato chip co-operative. In her account of the formation of the cable co-operative, Darlene described how the Co-operative Council played a similar role of gathering people together: 'The Co-operative Council ... that's the first place I went actually. I talked to Claudette [McNeill] personally and she said we should gather up a few people around the table to see what they think. So that's what we did.'

In addition to assisting with the formation of specific co-operatives, the Co-operative Council continues to play this animating role through such activities as the publication of a weekly community bulletin, which provides information about co-operative activities, and through the sponsorship of special events such as Co-op Week. The results of this work have been impressive. According to Claudette McNeill, the Co-operative Council was instrumental in the development of all the co-operatives formed in the Evangeline region since the mid-1980s. The means utilized to stimulate this development were 'education and the continual promotion of the co-operative philosophy' (Hammond Ketilson et al. 1992, 93).

As well, community development organizations have institutionalized and socialized the formation and development process. Both the Co-operative Council and the St Thomas Aquinas Society provided developmental assistance to the organizing committees of the new co-operatives. The St Thomas Aquinas Society, through the work of its development officer, was particularly active in the organization of Les P'tits Acadiens, and the Co-operative Council assisted with the incorporation of all the co-operatives. With the P.E.I. Potato Chip Co-operative it arranged meetings, obtained information, and arranged member training. With Les P'tits Acadiens, it handled the bookkeeping for the first few months. However, it was with the Community Communications Co-operative that the council was most actively involved. Unlike other co-operatives where the co-ordinating role was limited to the start-up period, with this co-operative the Council was involved with ongoing management and administration as well. This included surveys to determine community interest, the recruitment of members, the installation of the system, the preparation of budgets, and even day-to-day administration. Referring to the organizing role played by the Co-operative Council, Gilles Painchaud stated that: 'The council kind of took on the responsibility of getting it set up and getting the members.' The management and administrative roles played by the council are described as well by Claudette McNeill: 'For the cable co-op we did everything from A to Z. We made the contacts for the companies to come and install the system. If there was some material missing we had to order it. And then recruiting the members ... devising a system of how they were to pay their cable. We did that.'

While the Co-operative Council did not have the mandate to provide consulting services to member co-operatives to deal with their operational problems, the closeness of its association with the Community Communications Co-operative meant that the council could hardly avoid this kind of involvement. When it became clear that the cable co-operative was not moving to realize its original objectives and plans, the council assumed an interventionist role. It arranged for the hiring of a local consultant to make recommendations to the co-operative's board of directors regarding the actions that should be taken. The council then obtained the approval of the cable co-operative's board of directors for a working committee of ten community members to examine the report and recommend a course of action. Gilles Painchaud explained the need for this action as follows: 'It [the cable co-op] was not getting anywhere so they hired a consultant to prepare a plan.' As a follow-up to this action, the council, with the agreement of the board, arranged for funding to hire a project person to source the external funds required to implement the agreed-upon plan.

Another function performed by the Evangeline region community development organizations was the pooling of local financial resources and expertise. Both the Evangeline Credit Union and the Baie Acadienne Venture Capital Group provided financial assistance to the new co-operatives. The Baie Acadienne Venture Capital Group, sometimes in conjunction with provincial agencies, made seed grants available to the organizing committees of the co-operatives so that they could obtain the information necessary to proceed with their planning. This kind of assistance was provided to the P.E.I. Potato Chip Co-operative to send representatives to study potato chip plants in Pennsylvania as well as to Les P'tits Acadiens to attend the Canadian Festival of Fashion in Toronto.

In addition to assisting financially with the organization of the co-operatives, both the Evangeline Credit Union and the Baie Acadienne Venture Capital Group contributed in a major way to the operational financing of the co-operatives. In the case of the potato chip co-operative this amounted to a total of $420,000 from the Evangeline Credit Union ($200,000 in the form of a loan and $220,000 in preferred shares), while the Baie Acadienne Venture Capital Group contributed $51,000 in equity financing. For the cable co-operative, the loan from the Evangeline Credit Union amounted to $56,140, while the Baie Acadienne Venture Capital Group provided $60,500. In the case of Les P'tits Acadiens, the

Evangeline Credit Union initially provided a $15,000 business loan. When the co-operative ran into difficulty after six months, it applied for a further loan of $25,000, which was refused. Instead the Evangeline Credit Union offered to provide personal loans to individual members of the co-operative subject to the condition that their husbands acted as co-signers of the loans.

While the Industrial Commission did not provide project funding to the co-operatives, it assisted their start-up through the provision of expertise to help with the preparation of feasibility studies and business plans. The Evangeline Credit Union and the Baie Acadienne Venture Capital Group also provided expertise. For the P.E.I. Potato Chip Co-operative, expertise was provided through the non-voting membership of the Evangeline Credit Union on the co-operative's board of directors.

In addition to their community education, co-ordination, and resource pooling functions, the Evangeline region community development organizations have been a means of linking the region to external resources. The Co-operative Council, the St Thomas Aquinas Society, and the Industrial Commission were all useful in assisting the new co-operatives to access necessary external resources. The council was able to obtain funding on several occasions that allowed the cable co-operative to hire project workers and consultants. The Industrial Commission was able to negotiate successfully with provincial agencies for the substantial supplementary financing required for the construction of the potato chip factory and the purchase of equipment. The St Thomas Aquinas Society through their economic development officer assisted Les P'tits Acadiens to obtain training grants from Employment and Immigration Canada and financing for machinery and building rental from provincial agencies. The value of this linking function is illustrated by the work of the Co-operative Council in arranging for Chez Nous to receive a charitable tax number from Revenue Canada. After an initial refusal from Revenue Canada, the council contacted the Conseil canadien de la coopération, the apex organization for French-language co-operatives. As a result of lobbying by this national body, the refusal was changed to acceptance.

While the community development organizations were important in accessing external assistance, their value in gathering local
financial resources and expertise should not be forgotten. Without the loans and equity investments provided by the Evangeline
Credit Union and the Baie Acadienne Venture Capital Group, the
new co-operatives would have been unable to access the additional financing required. It was the leveraging effect of the
commitments made by the Evangeline region's own financial
institutions that allowed external financial institutions to participate.

Limitations of Community Development Organizations

While the Evangeline region community development organizations played a significant role in the formation of the co-
operatives, certain deficiencies in the organizations limited their
effectiveness in assisting the co-operatives' development. The
level of human and financial resources available to these organizations was inadequate. During the time these four co-operatives
were formed, the only full-time development position in the
Evangeline region was that of the manager of the Co-operative
Council. While the Industrial Commission has recently acquired a
full-time staff position with secretarial support and a small
project budget, a reduction in the grant to the Co-operative Council from the Department of the Secretary of State has necessitated
that the manager's position be cut back to part-time. Also, since
the Co-operative Council not only lacks a project budget but even
the resources to employ a secretary, much of the manager's time
is spent typing the community bulletin and on other routine
administrative tasks. Claudette McNeill outlined some of the constraints upon her work as follows: 'Out of the last three days ... at
least 95 per cent of my time was spent doing secretarial work,
because I don't have a secretary.' Also the national and international interest in the Evangeline region co-operatives has meant
that a good deal of her time is taken up with visitors. 'In the summer, we have a lot of people coming. I spend days sometimes
touring people around.'

As for the other community development organizations, the Baie Acadienne Venture Capital Group does not have paid staff, nor does the Evangeline Credit Union designate staff time for development work. As for the St Thomas Aquinas Society, it ceased to employ an economic development officer after the organization of the Baie Acadienne Industrial Commission. The lack of resources available to the community development organizations has meant that they do not have the capacity to provide the kind of developmental support to the region's co-operatives that is desirable. Many things that are needed just don't get done. Claudette McNeill described a number of education activities that she would like to initiate if the Co-operative Council had the resources to do so: 'There should be a director's training for all the boards of the co-operatives. Then for new members coming in there should be some kind of a basic course. And then all sorts of promotional activities for the public. And maybe something for the employees of the co-operatives. It's what I was saying about doing some development, some education. There isn't enough being done.'

While the community development organizations have supported the start-up of co-operatives, they have not acted to ensure their development and survivability. In considering the difficulties encountered by Les P'tits Acadiens, Carmella Richard wondered whether the Co-operative Council could have played a more constructive role in helping that business to solve its problems: 'Maybe the Co-operative Council should have organized things so that the co-operatives down here got together to talk about our problems. We all had our problems but we couldn't share. We were all there in our own different corners.'

Claudette McNeill admitted that the Co-operative Council has not provided assistance to co-operatives to deal with operational concerns. She further indicated that the region's co-operatives don't think of the Co-operative Council as being able to provide that kind of assistance: 'They don't come here if they have problems at all. I don't know how you could say it, but there's definitely something lacking. They don't think we can do anything or else they'd come ... I suppose if I had more time I could go and visit.' She believes, however, that the community development organizations should be given a broader mandate, which would involve them in monitoring the activities of the region's co-operatives, and in providing consulting services as required: 'The council is helpful to organize meetings, get things started, help co-operatives with their by-laws and incorporation and stuff like that, but there should be more. You know it would be nice if you had someone that could follow a co-operative ... attend their meetings, check their figures ... You know an advisor ... So what I would like to see is for the council to follow a co-op more closely and as soon as they think there might be a little problem or they might benefit from a better marketing plan, get Co-op Atlantic down here to do that.'

In addition to a low level of resources and a mandate that did not include operational support to existing co-operatives, the effectiveness of the community development organizations may have been limited by lack of staff experience and expertise. Claudette pointed out that one of the weaknesses of co-operative development was that sometimes things were done too quickly without enough consideration of alternatives: 'The people were so enthused about forming another co-operative that the long-term aspects of the enterprise on a business level were not given enough consideration. That is the reason why some of them failed' (Hammond Ketilson et al. 1992, 93). According to Claudette, if the staff 'had been well versed in community economic development,' they might have been more effective in helping organizing committees to foresee and avoid potential difficulties. This lack of local expertise has been particularly evident in relation to Les P'tit Acadiens and the P.E.I. Potato Chip Co-operative, both of which produced for markets external to the Evangeline region. Since the staff of the development organizations have not had training or experience related to production and marketing, they were unable to offer useful start-up advice, let alone operational advice. Leonce Bernard believes that this is still the case. Referring to the Co-operative Council, he stated that it 'doesn't have the capability at the moment to be involved in restructuring or really assisting co-operatives in an ongoing way.'

5. ROLE OF EXTERNAL AGENCIES AND ORGANIZATIONS

Provincial and federal governments assisted the formation and development of the co-operatives through the provision of community development staff, project development grants, project funding (for training, equipment, and buildings), and human resource expertise. This assistance, when it was responsive to community needs and was provided in a manner that was accountable to the organization, was perceived to have had a constructive effect that strengthened local organizations. Government assistance was perceived to have had a destructive effect when it was linked to fixed and inappropriate criteria, when it weakened local organizations, and when the community had little control over the quality of the aid received.

The provincial government played a community development function in the formation of Chez Nous, similar to that provided to the other co-operatives by the Evangeline community development organizations. Acting as a co-ordinator, Amand Arsenault, the director of the Regional Services Centre, encouraged members of the Chez Nous organizing committee to proceed with their ideas, assisted them to structure a wider planning group that contained the best local expertise, and worked to access appropriate government resources, both financial and human. Since he viewed himself as a resource person to the community, who acted under the direction of community members to access government services, Amand presented himself as a model of a democratically accountable public servant. From his perspective the role of government staff located in the Evangeline Regional Services Centre should be one of active participation in community projects: 'They can't be just giving out information. They have to be involved in what's taking place. The Regional Services Centre is a tool for development.' Certainly the government services provided by Amand had a positive impact upon the formation and development of Chez Nous. However, it is open to question whether this kind of government involvement is likely to be effective when, unlike Amand, the staff person is not at the same time a trusted community member.

Governments also assisted constructively in the formation of co-operatives through the provision of project development 'seed money.' Without such assistance neither the Co-operative Council (funded by the Department of the Secretary of State) nor the Industrial Commission (funded by the P.E.I. Department of Industry) would have been available to promote and initiate co-operative formation. In the early stages of their formation, small development grants to obtain the information necessary for business planning were particularly useful to the P.E.I. Potato Chip Co-operative and to Les P'tits Acadiens. At later stages such grants were useful to allow the co-operatives to hire their own co-ordinators, project staff, and consultants. The grant from the Department of Community and Cultural Affairs to the cable co-operative allowed for the hiring of a consultant whose report provided an essential framework for the co-operative to make decisions. The grant from the Department of Industry's Co-operative Development Fund allowed Chez Nous to hire as its own co-ordinator a person with the expertise to locate additional funding, negotiate the mortgage, and arrange for the construction of the building. As Amand Arsenault stated: 'We managed to get $5,000 out of the fund to hire a co-ordinator, and it did a lot of good. We should have maybe put it in place six months earlier.'

Governments also provided partial funding for the purchase of equipment, for building construction, and for training. This funding, while necessary, was sometimes made available in ways that limited its usefulness. It was helpful when it was a supplement to the commitment of community resources and when it assisted the co-operatives to achieve their objectives. It was harmful when it unduly influenced the co-operatives' planning and direction.

The government of Prince Edward Island invested substantially in the P.E.I. Potato Chip Co-operative. In addition to the $90,000 raised by worker-members and the $471,000 invested by Evangeline's community development organizations, the government of P.E.I. invested $570,000, of which $450,000 was a loan and $120,000 a grant. Over the years, the government has made additional investments so that its total investment was $800,000. While the amount of funding provided by government to Les

P'tits Acadiens was much less, it was significant. Whereas the worker-members of Les P'tits Acadiens originally contributed only $5,000, with $15,000 from the community development organizations, the government of P.E.I. provided a total of $40,000, of which $15,000 was forgivable if the co-operative operated for at least three years. In addition the government provided several thousand dollars in subsidy assistance for the rental of the workshop. (The workers contributed an additional $25,000 when the co-operative was restructured after the first year of operation.)

In addition to financing assistance for the capital costs of these projects from the provincial government, both Les P'tits Acadiens and Chez Nous received training grants from the federal government. In the case of Les P'tits Acadiens, worker-members received fifty weeks of paid training, while for Chez Nous a construction training project was approved for a maximum of $135,000. Chez Nous also received a $100,000 grant from the Fisheries Alternative Program of the federal Atlantic Canada Opportunities Agency, on the basis of the permanent jobs that it would create in the community. The cable co-operative also applied for government funding to expand the cable system together with the establishment of a community television capability and a mini-recording studio. However, as the federal government had recently suspended its support for community television, no funding was forthcoming.

While different types of government funding described in the previous paragraphs usually supplemented financing from the Evangeline region in necessary and useful ways, it sometimes had a limiting and even damaging effect upon the development of the co-operatives. This is seen most clearly in the case of Les P'tits Acadiens. While the project was still in the planning stage, the organizing committee applied for and received a training grant that committed the members to immediately begin full-time training on the job. To do this it was necessary to purchase equipment and set up a factory operation. Since the forgivable performance loan offered by the P.E.I. Development Corporation required the purchase of new equipment, Les P'tits Acadiens was forced to lay out more capital than was really necessary. Colette

Arsenault stated: 'We couldn't buy second-hand equipment which was available at the time and still get the forgivable performance loan. We had to buy new equipment.'

In effect the conditions attached to the training project and the P.E.I. Development Corporation loan had significantly influenced the planning of the project and the intentions of the organizing committee. They were no longer free to consider alternative ways to structure their project or to use their own common sense with respect to what they thought would work. Instead they were rushed into a full-time, factory-type mode of production, which was both costly in terms of overhead and which conflicted with their roles as mothers of young children. Colette Arsenault described the negative impact that the program criteria had upon the project: 'To get all those loans we had to set up in a shop somewhere. We couldn't do it from home. I think if the government hadn't been involved, and we could have bought the equipment second-hand and gone for piecework from home, we would probably have been able to swing it.'

Governments also supported the formation and development of the co-operatives through the provision of human resource expertise. Both Chez Nous and Les P'tits Acadiens utilized the technical expertise of information specialists with widely differing results. In the case of Chez Nous, the organizing group had a clear understanding that they were in charge. Referring to those persons who provided assistance to the project, Lorraine Arsenault said: 'They gave us the pros and cons. We made the decisions.' In the case of Chez Nous the organizing committee sought out the best local expertise to help them, and thereby expanded to a planning committee of twenty-two persons. As their co-ordinator and resource person, Amand Arsenault sought out appropriate government expertise when they required it. One example was a resource person from the Department of Health and Social Services, who assisted them to prepare a questionnaire and organize a survey. Another was a community planner who prepared a preliminary sketch of the building. In both situations the information received was appropriate and helped the planning group to move toward its goals.

With Les P'tits Acadiens, where the organizing committee relied more heavily on technical experts external to the community, the experience was very different. One consultant supplied by the Federal Business Development Bank to assist with on-the-job training was unsuitable since his only experience was with large clothing manufacturers in Montreal. Another consultant from the same organization encouraged the co-operative to purchase clothing fabric in bulk before the preparation and market testing of clothing samples. When sample prototypes were produced, the material was found to be unsuitable and had to be sold at a loss. In another situation the P.E.I. Development Corporation supplied a consultant to prepare designs for a new Anne of Green Gables line of children's clothing. After the designs had been prepared, the co-operative found that the sizes and proportions were wrong because the consultant had no familiarity with children's clothing.

Even worse was the experience with a consultant who visited three times at a cost to the co-operative of several thousand dollars and produced a report that was neither practical nor helpful. Colette Arsenault expressed her frustration with the often conflicting and inappropriate advice that the co-operative had received from externally supplied technical experts: 'We all paid for it. We had experts that were supposed to be there to help us out ... but there was nobody in the garment industry. We were getting advice from a lot of people. There came a point in time when there were too many people involved.'

Unlike Chez Nous, where the planning committee contained much of the expertise required to develop the project, none of the members of the Les P'tits Acadien's organizing group had the expertise relevant to either clothing manufacturing or the operation of a business. Consequently they lacked confidence in their own judgment, which placed them in a dependent position in relation to government consultants who were not accountable to the co-operative. The dependency of Les P'tits Acadiens upon external experts and the feeling of lack of control that the members experienced was emotionally described by Colette: 'We didn't know. We were going with what people were telling us because we thought they were the experts. And it took us almost a year to ... take things into our own hands ... But that was the year we lost a whole lot of money.'

In addition to their involvement with government agencies, Les P'tits Acadiens and the P.E.I. Potato Chip Co-operative were also involved to a limited extent with Co-op Atlantic around the marketing of their products. Without laying blame on one side or the other, the relationship that existed between these worker co-operatives and Co-op Atlantic did not work well for any of the parties. In terms of Les P'tits Acadiens, the relationship was fraught with misunderstanding from the beginning, so that a mutually agreed upon business arrangement was never established. Colette described some of the incidents that led Les P'tits Acadiens' frustration with Co-op Atlantic: 'They had a show in Moncton. I took all our clothes there. They were supposed to put them on display. They didn't ... We went to the co-operative stores. And they did buy some [children's clothing] the first year. But Co-op Atlantic was angry because we had gone directly to the co-ops.'

The P.E.I. Potato Chip Co-operative's relationship with Co-op Atlantic started out on a more positive note. Negotiations during the first year of operation led to an agreement with Co-op Atlantic to market the product under the co-op label. This agreement was retracted within a few months after Co-op Atlantic began to receive customer complaints about the chips. From the perspective of the potato chip co-operative, this action had serious consequences. In order to locate new markets, the potato chip co-operative was forced to set up its own expensive sales distribution network. This step, which greatly increased costs, contributed to the co-operative's ongoing financial difficulties and to the eventual decision to seek receivership protection. The specialized skills and services of Co-op Atlantic would have been helpful to Les P'tits Acadiens and the P.E.I. Potato Chip Co-operative if they had been accessible at critical junctures in the life of these co-operatives. Claudette McNeill argued: 'Co-op Atlantic has the capability of doing that. It has the resources both financial and human. They are doing it for consumer co-ops now and for housing co-ops through Atlantic People's Housing. But the other co-ops don't have access to their services.'

After the P.E.I. Potato Chip Co-operative went into receivership, it negotiated a business arrangement with Co-op Atlantic characterized by greater mutual accountability. This included an agreement by Co-op Atlantic to provide financial and marketing expertise, as well as to become a member (along with the Credit Union Central of P.E.I.) of the potato chip co-operative's board of directors. One wonders whether this arrangement could become a development model for the relationship between small emerging co-operatives and large established organization such as Co-op Atlantic.

6. MANNER OF PROJECT PREPARATION

While all four co-operatives sought to become financially viable, the way in which they developed and the resources available to them impacted upon their sustainability. The wide membership base of the service co-operatives meant that they offered far more opportunities for community participation than did the worker co-operatives. This was especially true in the operation phase of the co-operatives, but was true to some extent in the planning phase as well. During the planning and formation period, all four co-operatives recruited volunteers for their organizing and planning committees. For Chez Nous, the Community Communications Co-operative, and the P.E.I. Potato Chip Co-operative this resulted in broad community membership on the planning committee, while for Les P'tits Acadiens, membership was limited to a small group of the initiators' friends. Community meetings were used to encourage community participation. In the case of the service co-operatives, public meetings were held both to share information and to make decisions. Chez Nous' first public meeting and press conference, attended by some fifty people, presented the co-operative's general plans and objectives. At the second public meeting, those in attendance were involved in the decision to proceed or not to proceed with the building. In the case of the cable co-operative, the decision to block M1 Rural Television and Cable Systems' application for a licence and to investigate the possibility of setting up a co-operative was decided at the annual meeting of the Co-operative Council attended by some sixty people. In the case of the worker co-operatives, public meetings or press conferences were held solely to provide information. There was no opportunity for public decision-making. Thus Les P'tits Acadiens had a press conference to announce its plans, while the P.E.I. Potato Chip Co-operative held a very large public meeting (attended by about 125 people) to explain the co-operative's objectives and to solicit worker-members.

In addition to the recruitment of volunteers and the organization of public meetings, the community participated in the formation of the service co-operatives through attendance at social activities and special fund-raising events. In the case of the worker co-operatives this kind of community participation and support did not exist, because these projects were perceived to benefit individuals rather than the whole community. As a consequence of this lack of voluntary community support, the institutional support of the community development organizations was far more important to the worker co-operatives than to the service co-operatives, which received both voluntary and institutional community support.

After completion of the planning period, the community continued to participate actively in the affairs of the two service co-operatives while community-wide involvement with the two worker co-operatives decreased further. Chez Nous and the cable co-operative, with broadly based community memberships, were able to find new avenues for community participation. For Chez Nous this has meant the contribution of volunteer labour to build the centre and the promise of community members to spend time with seniors once the centre opens. For the cable co-operative it meant community decision-making around the plans for expansion. Les P'tits Acadiens and the P.E.I. Potato Chip Co-operative, because of their different membership structures, were operated by their members with little opportunity for community input. This limited involvement explains the relative lack of effort by community members to save Les P'tits Acadiens. Similarly when the potato chip co-operative was in crisis, help came not from the community but from the community development organizations. This suggests that the worker co-operative structure, based as it is on worker membership with potential benefits accruing primarily to the workers, cannot hope to receive broad community support in time of need. Unlike the potato chip co-operative, support for Les P'tits Acadiens was not forthcoming even from the development organizations. One wonders whether the community perception of Les P'tits Acadiens as a 'women's enterprise' may account for what appears to have been differential treatment.

All of the co-operatives attempted to gather local expertise to assist in the planning of the projects. Both of the service co-operatives were fortunate in that they were able to access most of the knowledge and skills they required in the community. The twenty-two members of the Chez Nous' planning committee brought skills ranging from kitchen design to building construction. The board of directors for the cable co-operative brought business expertise and, most important, a person with specialized knowledge in electronics. With the worker co-operatives, that was not the case. While the community had the leadership capacity to plan and organize these co-operatives, the specialized knowledge and skills required to produce goods for a competitive market was largely lacking.

Thus the P.E.I. Potato Chip Co-operative and Les P'tits Acadiens faced a double handicap in relation to the service co-operatives. They had neither a dependable community market nor the expertise to help them succeed in the wider market. Indeed the worker co-operatives not only lacked persons with appropriate technical expertise within the region but, as Colette Arsenault also pointed out with respect to Les P'tits Acadiens, this expertise was not even available in the province: 'We had experts that were supposed to be there to help us out ... but there was nobody in the garment industry ... There was no one but the teacher at Holland College, but she wasn't available to us.'

The P.E.I. Potato Chip Co-operative also lacked access to the necessary expertise. When the co-operative was having problems with product inconsistency, Eric Arsenault notes that the only source of help was the equipment manufacturer in Pennsylvania: 'I made a lot of calls to the States at first asking, "Why is it doing this? Why are we getting dark chips more than we should? And why are we getting big clumps of chips?" I believe we did lose some markets because of inconsistency of the product.'

The worker-members of Les P'tits Acadiens also lacked the necessary technical expertise in a variety of areas such as production, design, marketing, and business management. Consultants were obtained from government agencies to advise in these areas. Because the involvement of these experts with the co-operative was short-term and specific, they were not able to set in motion a learning process among the workers. Indeed the advice they provided was rarely helpful, and on occasion harmful. The underlying problem was that the co-operative did not have within it the necessary knowledge, skills, and experience required by the project. Les P'tits Acadiens' crash training program had underestimated what was required to operate successfully this clothing manufacturing enterprise. The manager lacked financial and marketing skills, while other members lacked production skills. Colette Arsenault sums up the problem: 'I didn't have the training. If I had to start a business again, I would go for six months at least and take a business course. I didn't know about finances and overhead and everything.' Carmella Richard agrees that experience and expertise was lacking: 'One setback for the co-operative was that there was nobody with enough experience. The biggest problem was that nobody was qualified to do the marketing.'

Members of the P.E.I. Potato Chip Co-operative also suffered from lack of knowledge and skills. While the manager had business training, he had no experience in the production of potato chips. The technicians were not licensed. To prepare for their tasks, they travelled to a United States plant for a week's training on how to make potato chips. According to Eric Arsenault, this training was far too short: 'We should have trained for six months.' Production-line workers and machine operators also lacked knowledge and skills. They received training on the job, but Eric believes that it would have been better for the co-operative if they had known how to do the job when the operation started: 'Education would have been the big thing at the start. We should have planned to have people that could do the job, or at least a budget for training these people. You have to know exactly what's going on. And this can only be achieved by training.'

Of the four co-operatives, Chez Nous, the cable co-operative and the potato chip co-operative have placed the most emphasis on planning for financial self-reliance. In the case of Chez Nous, there was a clear understanding that the construction of the centre would not proceed until sufficient financing had been obtained to achieve the project's goal of providing the service to seniors at an affordable cost. Consequently, the planning for the centre took place at a deliberate pace that was at times frustrating to the organizing committee. Before attempting to secure external funding, the initiators placed their emphasis upon first obtaining the financial support of the community. They set a target of $70,000, which was subsequently surpassed by an additional $40,000.

When financial support from the community was ensured, they began to investigate external sources of support. Some sources of financial support, such as Canada Mortgage and Housing Corporation, were rejected because of their restrictive program criteria. The first financial commitment received was a Section 25 grant from Employment and Immigration Canada to pay for the cost of labour during the construction phase. This grant might have stampeded them into an immediate decision to build, but they resisted that temptation. Instead a public meeting was called at which the financial implications of building with the money on hand were considered. As it would have been necessary to set rents at a level unaffordable to many seniors, the decision was taken not to proceed until additional financing could be obtained. This decision was reversed one month later after receipt of a grant from the federal Atlantic Canada Opportunities Agency as well as the confirmation of a long-term reduced-rate mortgage from L'Assomption Assurance. With a final budget based on known revenues and secure financing, and with rate levels that seniors can afford, the long-term viability of Chez Nous seems assured.

The cable co-operative has also emphasized planning for financial self-reliance. The decision to proceed was not taken until sufficient subscribers had been found to provide the operating revenue necessary to sustain the enterprise. Also all of the money to install the cable system and to purchase the equipment was raised locally. Based on expected monthly revenues from a set number of subscribers, the Evangeline Credit Union and the Baie Acadienne Venture Capital Group agreed to loan the co-operative the necessary funds. When costs of installation proved to be higher than the amount estimated, members of the co-operative's board of directors successfully directed their energies to finding additional subscribers. As Gilles Painchaud, the cable co-operative's first president, stated: 'This 170 members didn't come out of the blue. We called people ... We talked. We got somebody to go around house to house to explain to them what it was all about.' In 1991, the co-operative attempted to obtain external financing to pursue an ambitious expansion program that would have included not only an expansion of the cable system, but a community channel, and sound studio. Since external funding was unavailable, the co-operative was forced to modify its plans. Only the expansion of the cable system to smaller communities would proceed since this could be financed from subscription revenues and would not require large loans that could endanger the survival of the co-operative.

The P.E.I. Potato Chip Co-operative too emphasized planning for financial self-reliance, though with less success than the two service co-operatives. It proceeded deliberately with its plans to provide community employment through the creation of a manufacturing enterprise. Detailed information was gathered from other locations, and plans were carefully made in advance of the selection of the worker-members. Although the community at large did not contribute financially to this enterprise, both workers and community development organizations made significant contributions. These were used to leverage the additional funding required from external sources.

Unlike the two service co-operatives, however, with known revenues based on a secure community market, the potato chip co-operative faced the additional risks of establishing itself in an external marketplace. To minimize these risks a marketing manager was hired, a business plan was prepared, distribution channels arranged, and negotiations with Co-op Atlantic entered into. Yet in spite of the total support of Evangeline's community development organizations, as well as significant support from provincial government agencies, the potato chip co-operative was unable to capture the market share necessary to sustain itself as a self-reliant enterprise. In addition to the necessity of obtaining an adequate sales volume, the potato chip co-operative faced other barriers to self-reliance, which included the lack of operating capital, the impact of a severe recession, fire-sale pricing by large competitors, and the unforeseen emergence of the PVYN potato virus, which raised costs and lowered the demand for P.E.I. products. The experience of the P.E.I. Potato Chip Co-operative raises questions about the limits to policies of self-reliance and community control as well as the adequacy of the Evangeline region's community development organizations to provide the kind of assistance required by enterprises that must compete in the external marketplace.

Of the four co-operatives, the planning process of Les P'tits Acadiens appears to have been the least oriented toward financial self-reliance. While workers and community development organizations contributed to the project, the bulk of the start-up financing came from external sources. Instead of being guided by the goals of the project, it appears that the co-operative received direction from the grants it received. One of the significant characteristics of this project was the short interval from the beginning of planning to actual production. The co-operative was already operating just four months from the time the organizing group first started to meet. A second characteristic of this project was the integration of training with the operation of the co-operative. The on-the-job training grant linked training directly to production and necessitated a fast start-up of the operation. Once training commenced, the co-operative was operational even though project planning had not been completed, and little thought had been given to the establishment of a market. Wilfred Arsenault identified the haste with which the project was organized: 'Different contacts were made for suppliers and so on ... while the training was being done. So as soon as the training was done, the show went on the road.' Colette Arsenault summed up the impact of external programs upon the planning process: 'We should have waited, but the programs were there. Everything started falling into place so we just went ahead. And we weren't ready to start.'

The equipment grants and rental assistance received from the P.E.I. Development Corporation placed further constraints on the co-operative. Acceptance of the grants forced the co-operative into a full-time factory mode of production so that alternative ways of organizing the project could not be considered. The effect of this structuring was to saddle the co-operative with expensive overhead costs during the three or four months of the year that they didn't produce. In retrospect Colette recognized the effect that the grants had upon the co-operative's planning: 'All those grants look very good when you are starting and you don't know a whole lot. But I think if people want to start they should go small. We should have gone for piecework and tried to get our funding without government assistance, if we had to follow all those rules.'

Like the potato chip co-operative, Les P'tits Acadiens had to find a place in the competitive marketplace, but with even less readiness. The linkage of on-the-job training with the co-operative's operation meant that goods were being produced without purchase commitments by retailers or any certainty that they would attract consumer interest. While a limited survey of the need for children's clothing had been carried out, it did not provide an adequate basis for planning, since it was oriented only to the Evangeline region and did not identify specific customers. Colette stated: 'I think when it first got started, the survey was done in the region and not across the Island.' Even with production under way and no contracts in hand, the co-operative was unable to devote adequate resources to the marketing function. As a consequence, Colette noted much of their production remained unsold: 'There was nobody to do marketing for us. I would do some marketing ... but I had to help out with the production line. I helped with the pressing, packing, shipping and did the book work ... plus marketing.' Carmella Richard emphasized the same problem: 'There were not enough marketing strategies done. So after the first season we found we were in deep trouble. We were producing the clothing and then trying to sell it, which is a very bad thing.' While the adequacy of Les P'tits Acadiens' strategies of planning for financial self-reliance may be questioned, other factors also operated to limit the co-operative's chances for survival. As a worker co-operative, Les P'tits Acadiens also had to compete in a marketplace external to the community. Just as in the case of the P.E.I. Potato Chip Co-operative, neither the Evangeline region community development organizations nor government agencies were able to provide the linkage to the markets that the co-operative required.

In addition, Les P'tits Acadiens had to cope with gender-related barriers. Whether because it was a women's enterprise, and therefore not taken seriously, or for other reasons related to the nature of the enterprise itself, Les P'tits Acadiens did not receive the same level of support from the community development organizations as did the P.E.I. Potato Chip Co-operative. The leaders of the community organizations did not assist with its formation to the extent that they did with the potato chip co-operative. The Evangeline Credit Union not only denied Les P'tits Acadiens a second business loan, but at first insisted that the husbands of the members must act as co-signers. Finally, the community development organizations did not attempt to save this community business, when the members decided to shut it down. The restrictions attached to the funding from federal and provincial governments may also have been biased against women. As the co-operative was not able to consider a part-time, home-based style of operation, unnecessary conflict was created between members' roles as workers and their roles as mothers of young children. Colette Arsenault explained that this led to an under-standing within the co-operative, that if members were not prepared to work full-time, they must leave. This policy had unfortunate consequences for the co-operative: 'I stopped after two years because I was pregnant with my third child. And they did operate for three years after that. When they stopped, the manager, Carmella Richard, was pregnant with twins.' In the final analysis, the gender barrier may have been an important contributing factor to closure of Les P'tits Acadiens.

CONCLUSION

Evidence from the case histories showed that the Evangeline region people have combined institutional structures with volun-tary grassroots action to successfully promote the formation and development of co-operatives as a means for community-based development. Initiators and organizers of the four co-operatives studied were motivated by attitudes of attachment to the commu-nity and a perspective of community distinctiveness that grew out of the context of dense interpersonal linkages and historical struggle. Initiators' strong sense of attachment to community members and identification with their concerns resulted in atti-tudes of confidence. This confidence, which was based on trust that the community would respond in positive ways to initiatives that they might undertake, encouraged them to share their ideas with others, to form support groups, and to initiate action. The perspective of 'distinctiveness' provided a sense of direction that guided the activities of initiators and organizers. This direction was toward a type of development that would benefit the whole community and would value social and cultural needs equally with economic ones. Self-reliance was seen as the preferred means to attain this goal.

An examination of the activities carried out by initiators and other members of the organizing committees to elicit support from community members and organizations indicated that the co-operatives did not develop automatically from a base of cul-tural solidarity. To obtain community support, organizers and community development organizations employed a number of involvement strategies, which appealed both to members' identification with the community and to their individual interests. Thus they utilized as incentives both the benefits to be obtained by the community (additional employment, care of seniors) and benefits to be enjoyed by community members themselves (prizes, a job, entertainment) to obtain participation. This process of community involvement, through combining material incentives with solidary and purposive ones, not only succeeded in building the support necessary for the success of specific projects, but worked as well to maintain and deepen community linkages. Thus the formation and development of co-operatives often became community-building experiences that strengthened attachments and identifications.

The prominent role played by leaders holding paid positions in the community and by the community development organizations illustrates the importance of an institutional support base for the formation and development of co-operatives. The presence of a significant number of employment opportunities in government, cultural agencies, and co-operative organizations allowed the Evangeline region to retain and develop many of its leaders. In addition, the fact that community members were at the same time institutional leaders meant not only that other community members found it easy to approach them with ideas but also that these leaders brought both a personal and a professional commitment to their work. In practical terms this translated into collaborative efforts to overcome barriers and to obtain the resources necessary for implementation.

The primary contribution of the community development organizations has been to institutionalize the formation and development of co-operatives. Consequently the formation of new co-operatives no longer depends totally upon the spontaneous initiatives of community members. In the Evangeline region these organizations have demonstrated that they are both able to provide assistance to grassroots initiatives and, as in the case of the potato chip co-operative, to play an animating role to bring forth new ideas. In addition to their role of bringing people together and encouraging community participation, the community development organizations have acted to gather local financial resources, to provide start-up expertise, and to access external resources. While all of these activities have been helpful during the formation stage of a co-operative, the community development organizations have been limited in what they contribute to a co-operative's development and sustainability. These limitations are a function of the community development organizations' low level of human and financial resources, lack of business expertise, and inadequate mandate for involvement in the operating difficulties of the region's co-operatives.

In some instances external agencies played important constructive roles, while in other situations they were ineffective or even destructive. Government assistance that was responsive to co-operatives' needs, as in the provision of a grant to Chez Nous to hire a co-ordinator, was useful. On the other hand, the rigid criteria attached to the assistance received by Les P'tits Acadiens was harmful. Similarly, government assistance that was provided in a accountable way and that helped the organizing group to develop its capacity, as in Amand Arsenault's work with Chez Nous, was helpful. Assistance that only confused the organizing group and left it feeling a lack of control, as in Les P'tits Acadiens' many experiences with consultants, had a destructive effect. The lack of specific worker co-operative legislation, which inhibited the potato chip co-operative from accepting new members, also had a damaging effect. With respect to the relationships of Evangeline's co-operatives with Co-op Atlantic, the lack of a framework specifying mutual responsibilities was damaging to both Les P'tits Acadiens and the potato chip co-operative. The revised arrangement, specifying as it did, responsibilities and commitments on the part of both Co-op Atlantic and the potato chip co-operative, might serve as a development model for emerging co-operatives.

In terms of the way projects are developed, it was noted the service co-operatives with community-based membership are more likely to receive widespread community support than worker co-operatives that must depend for support on institutional mechanisms. Also it was seen that a self-reliant approach, which emphasized community involvement, has been effective where projects depend upon community loyalty to succeed. Where projects must survive in the open marketplace, community-level strategies of self-reliance were inadequate. The need for market access, specialized expertise, and worker training suggests the importance of partnership arrangements with larger organizations to obtain the required resources.

4

A Theoretical Framework

Using the analysis of the case studies as the primary data, a theoretical framework of community economic development now is proposed. There are three essential elements: community consciousness, empowering activities, and supportive structures. This framework (Elements for a Framework of Community Economic Development) is depicted in the figure on page 120.

The three essential elements – community consciousness, empowering activities, and supportive structures – are shown in the left-hand column of the figure and elaborated upon in the middle column. For example, components of a community consciousness are community attachments and a movement perspective; empowering activities include involvement strategies and strategies of self-reliance; and supportive structures include community development organizations from the local community and external agencies such as government and central cooperative organizations.

ELEMENT 1. COMMUNITY CONSCIOUSNESS

A. Community Attachments

The first component of community consciousness is community attachments. The connection that the Acadian people feel to each other and to the Evangeline region is one of the paramount explanatory factors for community economic development.

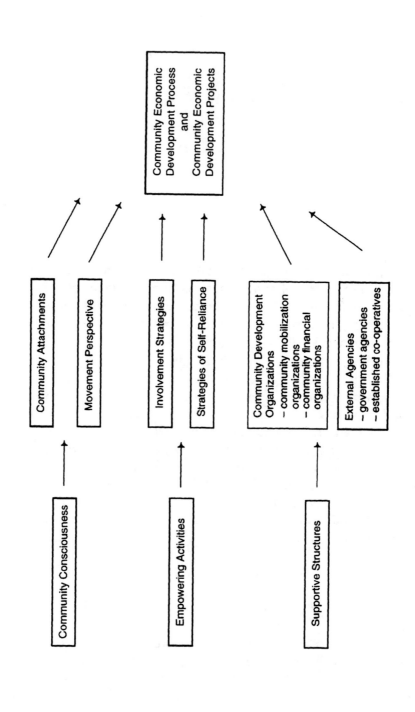

Attachments to family and friends through social networks, to other community members through social organizations, and to the territorial base itself, provide project initiators and members of planning committees with the energy to act. The motivation of initiators can be explained by their integration into supportive community networks. Solidary bonds with other community members provide the 'pull' that has moved community members to action (McAdam 1982). This 'pull' has worked in two ways: First, the existence of interpersonal attachments has meant that Olson's (1965) free-rider problem has been reduced, because while community members may benefit from a community project regardless of their personal participation, their friendship bonds act as a force 'pulling' them towards involvement. Second, it has meant that initiators experienced community needs as their own through connecting their self-interest as persons to the interest of their group. With Chez Nous and the cable co-operative, initiators connected their own personal welfare with that of the region's seniors and cable subscribers. Attachments to the community were also important for the P.E.I. Potato Chip Co-operative and Les P'tits Acadiens, in that persons who did not intend to become worker-members assisted. In addition to friendship they wanted to contribute to the creation of employment opportunities for their region.

The findings also support McAdam's (1982) research, which shows that supportive networks in which communication takes place freely are conducive to the development of a sense of confidence. Initiators of the Evangeline co-operatives believed that their efforts could make a difference. The ideas for all four co-operatives came out of the lived experience of community members. Project initiators who came forward with ideas trusted that community members and institutional leaders would respond supportively. Acting on this expectation, they shared their ideas with others, formed support groups, and proceeded to implement their ideas.

The feelings of community solidarity displayed by the initiators of the Evangeline co-operatives are necessary for an alternative economic paradigm in which the economy would exist to promote community (see Daly and Cobb 1990, for example). Hirschman (1970) refers to such feelings as 'loyalty,' which has the power to generate 'voice.' In the Evangeline region initiators clearly understood the importance of utilizing loyalty to meet community needs. The organizers of Chez Nous realized that they could only expect broad public support if it was clear that the purpose of the project was primarily for community benefit rather than to benefit its workers. Consequently they switched from the idea of a worker co-operative to a service co-operative with a community-wide membership. Experience from the other co-operatives supported the wisdom of their choice. The worker co-operatives (the P.E.I. Potato Chip Co-operative and Les P'tits Acadiens), which were structured to benefit only the worker-members, did not receive the level of community support enjoyed by co-operatives with wider memberships.

The prominence of community attachments in the formation of the Evangeline co-operatives suggests that this factor must be taken seriously because initiators need to be able to rely on each other and the community. If supportive networks are lacking they must be created because it is understood that projects with a broad-based appeal have the best chance of producing community loyalty.

B. Movement Perspective

Movement perspective, the second component of community consciousness, is as essential to community economic development as community attachments. It has arisen from an understanding that members of the Evangeline community were not simply individuals of Acadian descent but were part of an Acadian nation. A movement perspective is an awareness of a collective difference; of distinctive needs and aspirations, which grow out of a common cultural, geographic, or socio-economic background. Such an awareness may be described as a critical consciousness that, in Evangeline, existed not only among community leaders but at the popular level as well. Jösch (1983) also found that such an awareness, including knowledge of socio-economic relationships, was critical to co-operatives developing a common perspective that directed and energized them.

The Evangeline movement perspective emphasized that the community good had precedence over private interests, that social, cultural, and economic needs were indivisible, and that the realization of these values required collective, democratically guided local effort. Such a vision has a good deal in common with Robert Owen's ideal of a co-operative community. While the movement perspective in Evangeline also shared some ideals in common with other co-operatives (for example, such values as equality and mutual self-help), this perspective went beyond the specific forms of contractual co-operation (see Craig 1993), found in most co-operative organizations, to articulate a broader vision involving the unity of the social, cultural, and economic, more typical of comprehensive models of co-operation. The movement perspective in Evangeline meant that 'expressive rationality,' the human aspect of co-operation, was as important as 'instrumental rationality,' the business aspect of co-operation (Ekelund 1987, 15).

A movement perspective supported community economic development in the Evangeline region in several ways. First, it legitimized community resistance to development that was externally owned and controlled. The widespread understanding of the necessity to retain the region's cultural identity translated into a general acceptance that struggle and effort were required to preserve what was considered valuable. As an illustration, the cable co-operative was organized to prevent an external company from providing cable service. Also the planning committee for Chez Nous refused to consider an outside entrepreneur's proposal to build and operate a seniors' facility. In these ways a movement perspective supported endogenous development.

Secondly, a movement perspective supported community economic development by providing a direction that was broader than one that was strictly economic. The purpose of community economic development in Evangeline was to pursue the common good of the region (the goal of equity), taking into account social and cultural needs as well as economic ones. Such a view differed fundamentally from the model suggested by the Economic Council of Canada (1990), which equated community economic development with job creation. The Evangeline approach was more akin to visions of development articulated by community economic development theoreticians such as MacLeod (1989), who speaks of 'redressing exploitation,' or Bryant (personal communication, 14 Feb. 1992), who speaks of 'the empowerment of people through the development of a critical analysis and the ownership and control of economic structures.' In fact the Evangeline view of development calls into question mainstream economic approaches and is closer to notions of 'alternative development' that have arisen from experience in the Third World. According to these ideas genuine development must recognize the interdependencies between economic reasoning and the moral relations that link people to each other, and market values must be linked to a community's social values (Friedmann 1992). Within this paradigm the purpose of community economic development is no longer strictly economic. It is to empower people through building accountable structures of social power at the community level.

Finally, the ideas of cultural resistance and struggle contained within a movement perspective point to the importance of creating community-controlled institutions that are both accountable and culturally appropriate. Since Evangeline residents could not depend upon mainstream political, social, and economic institutions to preserve what they valued, they were forced to rely upon themselves. Instead of submission and cultural disintegration, the oppression that they experienced engendered opposition which they channelled into institution-building. To achieve this result, they chose the route of social entrepreneurship. That is, they pooled their resources and risked them collectively in democratically structured organizations. Through this participatory learning process they developed their capacities and sustained the vitality of their community.

It was not accidental that Evangeline has utilized social entrepreneurship for the provision of basic services required by residents of the region. The region was influenced by the Antigonish

Movement that swept through the Maritimes in the 1930s, which left an enduring influence ever since through the work of such organizations as the St Francis Xavier Extension Department. Although Antigonish has had a general impact throughout Atlantic Canada, its impact was greater in communities such as Evangeline than in others. For example, the 'kitchen table' meeting tradition of Antigonish was maintained in Evangeline and was used by the community in the initiation process for the P.E.I. Potato Chip Co-operative. In part this might be because Evangeline represented fertile ground for Antigonish. Evangeline had roots for social entrepreneurship that went back to the 1860s when farmers in the region were creating seed grain banks such as the Rustico Farmers' Bank, which was a forerunner of French Canada's *caisses populaires* and English Canada's credit unions.

Therefore, the movement perspective has been vital to the process of community economic development. The movement perspective, with its emphasis on cultural survival and social entrepreneurship, has allowed the initiators of co-operatives to tap a broader range of human motivations than would have been possible by development for economic purposes alone (Friedmann 1992). Development in the Evangeline region was powered by the forces of community attachments (social bases of power) as much as by economic self-interest (instrumental basis of power). With Chez Nous, the dominant motivation was the welfare of the region's seniors; with the cable co-operative the preservation of the French language was paramount. Even with the two worker co-operatives, the P.E.I. Potato Chip Co-operative and Les P'tits Acadiens, employment of members was not the only incentive. Non-members participated on the planning committees to create additional employment for their community. In addition the logic of resistance contained in the movement perspective led to the formation of counter-institutions that have themselves become a further basis of social power.

Finally, the movement perspective has supported development because it kept the Evangeline people focused on goals beyond their own immediate community. Since they saw themselves as part of the Acadian nation, their aims included the well-being of that nation. These broader goals served as an antidote to community parochialism and the territoriality of community-interest groups. It connected them in solidarity not only with Acadians but also with French-language groups both across North America and throughout the world. The result has been a broadening of local horizons, one instance of which is Evangeline's involvement in international development through a co-operative that carries out projects in Haiti. The benefits of participation in a broader movement has also manifested itself concretely, as in the donations and low-interest mortgage for Chez Nous provided by L'Assomption Assurance, a Moncton-based French-language insurance company.

ELEMENT 2. EMPOWERING ACTIVITIES

A. Involvement Strategies

Empowering activities, the second essential element (see figure on page 120), may be divided into strategies of involvement and self-reliance. Involvement strategies, representing the approach that initiators and community development organizations took to obtain maximum possible community participation, find their source in the region's historical traditions of informal co-operation and mutual self-help. Such strategies are essential to community economic development because as the case studies demon-strated it is involvement mechanisms that both create community participation for particular projects and build long-term attachments to the community. In the Evangeline approach to community economic development, participation is not taken for granted but is encouraged in all community projects. Involvement strategies of a recreational and social nature are deliberately utilized to obtain participation. Initiators of the co-operatives appealed for community support on the basis of three types of incentives: individual benefit (material incentives), friendship (solidary incentives), and community loyalty (purposive incentives). They did not expect that solidary and purposive incentives alone would be sufficient to ensure participation. While Chez

Nous emphasized the well-being of senior citizens, it also used contests, prizes, and social gatherings to involve the community. The cable co-operative stressed the importance of French language and culture, but also described the benefits available to individual subscribers. In the worker co-operatives the purposive incentive of jobs for community members was mixed with the solidary incentive of working in a collective enterprise as well as the material incentive of employment for individuals.

In addition to the use of multiple incentives, an involvement orientation requires open democratic processes and structures. Initiators made every effort to inform the community about their ideas and to seek community support. With the help of the community development organizations they organized broadly based planning committees to ensure that project ownership was widely shared in the community. The P.E.I. Potato Chip Co-operative involved all relevant stakeholders, potential worker-members, farmers, and local financial institutions. Chez Nous made sure that its planning committee included representatives from each parish and municipality. To encourage community involvement, project information was disseminated widely through the weekly community bulletin, the provincial Acadian newspaper, *La Voix Acadienne*, press conferences and well-advertised public meetings. Door-to-door visitations and membership recruitment campaigns were common. For the cable co-operative, a membership drive provided the solution to a financial crisis. Perhaps most important of all, the nature of the co-operative structure meant that members had equal decision-making rights. For example, at the public meeting of 1 July 1992, against the recommendations of the planning committee, members voted to postpone construction of Chez Nous until additional funding could be arranged.

An involvement orientation also played an important role in sustaining community attachments and a movement perspective. First, efforts by initiators and community development organizations to involve the community in the initiation and planning of a new co-operative resulted in community support and participation. Second, the act of participation itself became a community-building experience. What happened was that participation in valued projects pulled the community together, so that attachments and perspectives were strengthened. Although this occurred to some extent in all four co-operatives, it was particularly evident in Chez Nous. Community members described their amazement at the way Chez Nous had brought the community together. They also cited the formation of the Evangeline Funeral Co-operative as another exceptional example of a participatory experience that had unified the Evangeline community.

These observations suggest that community interests may be socially constructed by the mobilization process itself, a point made by Jenkins (1983) and Hirsch (1986). Hirsch found that people not only get involved for different reasons but also that these reasons may change as a result of the process of mobilization. Persons who joined a block club or tenants' union to benefit themselves found that as a result of this experience social ties with other members became an additional incentive to participate. Persons who extended their participation beyond the neighbourhood organization to a community-level organization did so on the basis of reciprocity. The key incentive for this wider participation was loyalty to a community organizer from the central organization who had helped them in the past. Through participation at the level of the community organization, they began to identify with broader goals so that the well-being of the community now became an incentive. Hirsch's findings provide a useful framework for understanding the significance of an involvement orientation to the development of the Evangeline co-operatives.

The initiators of the co-operatives were already motivated by solidary and purposive incentives. They were closely linked to their community and could visualize the importance of the new organizations to the community's welfare. They personally recruited additional persons, some of whom shared their concerns and others who joined for reasons of personal benefit. As the projects developed, the planning committees organized activities and strategies to involve other members of the community. What this analysis suggests is that even in a culturally homogeneous region like Evangeline, participation is not automatic. It happens as a result of deliberate involvement efforts.

B. Strategies of Self-Reliance

Strategies of self-reliance, a second aspect of empowering activities, must also be considered essential to the success of community economic development in the Evangeline region. These strategies grew out of the popular conviction that local control of social and economic institutions was necessary to preserve the Acadian way of life. According to the manager of the P.E.I. Potato Chip Co-operative, self-reliant development through the co-operatives kept the community together and made possible the retention of the Acadian culture.

As defined in community development literature, self-reliance does not signify isolationism and self-sufficiency, as is commonly thought. Instead self-reliance 'aims to avoid becoming dependent by fostering both independence and interdependence' (Galtung, 103). According to Cossey (1990, 37), 'it means relying on local abilities, resources and judgement, while identifying a role for outsiders. It acknowledges the need for collaboration and partnership among various internal and external stakeholders.' Self-reliant strategies that supported the formation of the Evangeline region co-operatives included the local initiation and direction of projects, the utilization of local knowledge and skills, the mobilization of the community's financial resources, and the establishment of collaborative external relationships.

The self-initiated character of development in the Evangeline region was particularly striking. Community members took the responsibility to generate ideas and to propose solutions to community problems rather than waiting for some other body to take action. This proactive approach is described by Max-Neef (1991, 52) as 'revitalization through one's own efforts, capabilities and resources.' In what appears to be a common pattern, community members shared their concerns with close friends or others with whom they felt comfortable. Next they talked with community leaders, who encouraged them to meet with a wider group to discuss their ideas further. These informal meetings culminated in the recruitment of additional volunteers and the formation of planning committees to direct the projects. The establishment of the Co-operative Council institutionalized these self-reliant processes. Through the work of its manager, the Co-operative Council provided organizational support for the efforts of the initiators. With the P.E.I. Potato Chip Co-operative, the Council went one step further to initiate the needs-identification process itself. This was all achieved without external 'community developers.'

The utilization of the knowledge and skills of community members also promoted self-reliance. Initiators of the co-operatives selected the persons that they planned to recruit on the basis of the skills that the co-operatives needed. With Chez Nous and the cable co-operative they were able to find persons with relevant skills and experience who made contributions that were extremely important to the success of these organizations. Also through their participation in the decision-making process, these persons expanded their skills and broadened their knowledge. The practice of filling positions in the community (including government positions) with local people also supported self-reliance. The employment opportunities provided by the co-operatives as well as government and non-governmental cultural organizations allowed the Evangeline region to retain a critical mass of community leaders. As a result Evangeline possesses a leadership infrastructure that many rural communities lack.

The use of local knowledge and skills was less important in the formation of the worker co-operatives, Les P'tits Acadiens and the P.E.I. Potato Chip Co-operative. Initiators were unable to locate community members with the specialized skills these co-operatives required. This meant increased dependence upon external experts who prescribed solutions, and a resultant decrease in members' confidence in their ability to solve their own problems.

The mobilization of local financial resources by the Evangeline Credit Union and the Baie Acadienne Venture Capital Group also contributed to local control. The cable co-operative raised all its financing locally, either through memberships or through loans and grants from community financial organizations. It did not decide to proceed until sufficient commitments had been received from subscribers to cover the operating costs. Similarly, Chez Nous emphasized local responsibility. Loans and grants from external organizations were sought only after intensive fund-raising had taken place at the local level. The decision to build was only taken when it was certain that sufficient funding was available to cover the operating costs.

For the two worker co-operatives, the P.E.I. Potato Chip Co-operative and Les P'tits Acadiens, the achievement of financial self-reliance was much more difficult. Both attempted to use independent strategies, but since their primary market was external to the Evangeline region, community interdependence and loyalty were not sufficient to make their ventures successful. Instead of the horizontal relationships of mutual self-help within their community, they were forced to operate in an environment characterized by vertical instrumental relationships of power. The lack of any possibility of interdependence at this level had a serious impact upon their chances of success. Like the cable co-operative and Chez Nous, the potato chip co-operative sought to follow strategies of financial independence, although the scale of the project meant that it required financing far beyond the community's own capacity. This necessitated the balancing of community-level contributions with assistance from government. While the general community was barred from participating by the nature of the co-operative, worker-members made substantial commitments, as did the community financial organizations. In spite of these efforts, the co-operative faced two major limitations to self-reliance: its large external debt and the lack of partnership relationships with external organizations that were necessary to ensure a market for its product.

As a producer for an external market, Les P'tits Acadiens was also limited by its lack of interdependent relationships beyond the community. Even more important for Les P'tits Acadiens was its lack of financial independence. Les P'tits Acadiens placed much less emphasis than the other co-operatives on self-financing

and careful planning, as reflected in the minimal financial investment of the worker-members. While the Evangeline Credit Union
provided a loan, the main start-up financing came from an highly
attractive government training grant that may have shaped the
direction of the project. With the promise of a full year of paid
employment, the grant was almost too good to turn down. The
grant determined that the enterprise would be a full-time, factory
operation, and in effect disrupted the co-operative's planning
process before any thought had been given to something as fundamental as the markets for the products. Although Les P'tits
Acadiens intended to be self-reliant and independent, it seems
that the strategies actually utilized were dependent and grant
driven.

Self-reliance was also fostered through collaboration and partnerships, particularly within the local community. In the formation of the cable co-operative and Chez Nous, virtually all of the
community organizations contributed in one way or another.
Community goodwill also extended to the other co-operatives,
but their membership structure limited the possibility of support.
The extensive community support received by co-operatives with
broad community membership raises questions about the value
of worker co-operatives in this community. Perhaps a multi-
stakeholder approach (see Jordan 1989) representing both community members and employees might have been more effective,
as that structure would have provided the base of support from
the community that Chez Nous and the cable co-operative had.
Whether that would have been sufficient for these enterprises to
succeed is a debatable point because the worker co-operatives, as
noted, also related primarily to external markets whereas the
market for Chez Nous and the cable co-operative was from
within the region. Nevertheless, Evangeline does have successfully functioning co-operatives with markets external to the community (for example, the Acadian Co-operative Fishermen's
Association and the Acadian Pioneer Village), and in both cases
the membership base within the community is larger than for
either Chez Nous or the cable co-operative.

In reflecting upon the Evangeline region's strategies for self-reliance one first must be impressed by the responsibility that community members took to initiate their own development with the help of the Co-operative Council. With so many people having participated in the formation of co-operatives and in other community projects, there was a lot of local expertise available about how to form a new co-operative. With the P.E.I. Potato Chip Co-operative and Les P'tits Acadiens, what was missing was knowledge specific to the project. This suggests the need to organize specialized training well in advance of project start-ups. An important factor in Evangeline's self-reliance is the availability of local financial institutions that support community economic development. The role of the Baie Acadienne Venture Capital Group and the Evangeline Credit Union in accessing both local and external capital cannot be overemphasized. The failure of both worker co-operatives, however, suggests the need to minimize the risk of such projects for the community financial system.

ELEMENT 3. SUPPORTIVE STRUCTURES

A. Community Development Organizations

The third essential element, supportive structures, is subcategorized into two main components: community development organizations and external support organizations (see figure on page 120). Of the community development organizations, the Co-operative Council, the Evangeline Credit Union and the Baie Acadienne Venture Capital Group have been the most important. These organizations supported the initiatives of community members and leaders and encouraged the emergence of new initiatives. Essentially the community development organizations functioned as an institutional extension of voluntary community action. As such they effectively supported the formation of co-operatives through the promotion of community education and participation, the organization of local financial resources, the provision of development expertise, and the provision of links to external resources.

   While this study was consistent with other research that found that support organizations have a positive impact upon community economic development (Conte and Jones 1991; Cornforth et al. 1988; Whyte and Whyte 1988), the reasons for the effectiveness of Evangeline's community development organizations require further consideration. According to McCarthy and Zald's (1973) entrepreneurial theory of movement formation, the major explanatory factor in mobilization is the availability of resources, particularly leaders and organizing facilities. Other proponents of resource mobilization theory (for example, Jenkins 1983) argue that group organization and political opportunity should be included as additional factors. In the Evangeline region, the community development organizations focused local resources upon community economic development. The hiring of a full-time staff person for the Co-operative Council increased the ability of that organization to assist development in the region. In addition the acquisition of staff positions by the development organizations was a means of retaining leaders in the community. The establishment of the Baie Acadienne Venture Capital Group meant that both seed money to investigate ideas and risk capital to provide equity for new ventures were available. The organization of local resources through the mechanism of community institutions meant that ongoing information and animation processes could be carried out. Activity leading to co-operative development could be stimulated, and persons with ideas could be assisted to organize. Finally, the existence of the community development organizations allowed the community to take advantage of favourable political opportunities. With a cabinet minister at the provincial level who strongly supported co-operative development, and an expansion at the federal level of support for minority cultures such as the Acadian, the times were fortuitous. However, without organizations staffed by persons familiar with government programs and having the time to write proposals, the needed external assistance would not have been obtained.

Although this study found that the community development organizations were effective in supporting community economic development, it also identified limitations. The first was a lack of necessary human and financial resources. The staffing levels and range of staff expertise were inadequate. Also these organizations lacked discretionary funding that they could use for such things as training, the preparation of business plans, feasibility studies, and the hiring of project staff. The source of this limitation seems to have been the lack of recognition by governments of the potential of development organizations. With the exception of the Baie Acadienne Industrial Commission, which has recently received a full-time staff position, the community development organizations do not receive funding for community economic development. The small amount of federal funding available to the Co-operative Council comes by virtue of its cultural role rather than its development role. As a consequence of this lack of government recognition and support, the development organizations' activities and potential have been curtailed.

A second limitation was the inability of the community development organizations to assist the co-operatives beyond the formation period. With the possible exception of the cable co-operative (where the lack of a manager meant the Co-operative Council provided day-to-day administrative services), the community development organizations were of little help to co-operatives that encountered business difficulties. Some of the reasons for their ineffectiveness in sustaining these co-operatives included their lack of a mandate to monitor and to become involved in the co-operatives' affairs, their lack of the necessary management and business expertise, and their lack of access to the specialized resources of the broader co-operative system.

The Evangeline community and the co-operative system are jointly responsible for this second limitation. The co-ordinating role of the Evangeline Co-operative Council changed the Evangeline co-operatives from separate unifunctional organizations responsible only to their membership to a multifunctional co-operative group that considers issues from the perspective of the community. Without dissolving the vertical linkages of the individual co-operatives to their respective provincial-level centrals, the Co-operative Council formed horizontal linkages with all of the community-initiated co-operatives. As a result the Evangeline group of co-operatives came into being, with the capacity to consider development from the point of view of the community rather than solely from the point of view of each co-operative organization. Yet this new arrangement was a partial one. It did not establish operational linkages be-tween the co-operative organizations or provide the Co-operative Council with the authority to pursue further co-operative integration. Rather it created a proactive intermediary structure with the moral authority to provide leadership, but with no organizational authority. The Co-operative Council was not structured to allow participation in the affairs of an individual co-operative or to establish procedures for mutual self-help between the co-operatives. One member of Les P'tits Acadiens suggested that the inability of the Co-operative Council to make available the sales expertise of the Acadian Co-operative Fishermen's Association (an established fish processing and marketing co-operative in the community) to Les P'tits Acadiens illustrated the weakness of the Co-operative Council as a co-ordinator of resources. The linking of the Evangeline co-operatives through the Co-operative Council had provided a community viewpoint, but it did not establish an integrated system of mutual self-help between co-operatives.

To an even greater degree, the relationship of the Evangeline co-operatives to the overall co-operative system pointed out the absence of mechanisms of mutual self-help. The Evangeline production co-operatives were unable to access the advice and specialized skills from Co-op Atlantic that were needed for their operations to be successful. Yet mechanisms exist for Co-op Atlantic to provide services on a regularized basis to retail co-operatives across the Atlantic region that make up its membership. Its responsibility to its members makes it difficult for Co-op Atlantic to respond to the needs of other community-initiated co-operatives, such as the four cases studied in Evangeline.

Yet despite these limitations, the Co-operative Councils pioneered in Atlantic Canada by the Acadian communities of Evangeline, P.E.I., and Chéticamp, Nova Scotia, have been judged to be so successful that they are now being heralded as models for other Atlantic region communities. At the 1991 annual general meeting of Co-op Atlantic, delegates approved a broader vision for the organization ('A Proposal for Renewal'), which included support for the formation of locally based co-operative councils as a means of promoting community economic development. Since that time Co-op Atlantic, with the assistance of the Community Development Co-operative of Nova Scotia, has been instrumental in the formation of six such councils in various parts of Nova Scotia, and eleven additional councils have been formed in other parts of the Atlantic region (Roy, Dec. 1992, 1). Since the local communities have taken the lead role in the formation of these councils, the idea is apparently one that they find attractive. If some of the limitations observed in the Evangeline Co-operative Council can be removed, it is likely that the model can be even more effective.

B. External Support Organizations

External support organizations are government agencies and established co-operatives. Each of these will be discussed in turn.

Government Agencies

The contributions of governments to the formation of the Evangeline co-operatives, while important to projects designed to serve the community, and essential to projects with a focus beyond the community, have provided mixed benefits. Governments supported community economic development through the partial funding of the Evangeline development organizations, the provision of seed money to carry out studies and develop plans, the partial funding of projects, the co-ordinating roles played by staff, and by the provision of specialized resource persons. Yet this support has not always been helpful. The availability of funding sometimes led to a lack of self-reliant planning and created dependency upon government. This was particularly evident when the criteria attached to government funding imposed conditions upon the organizing committees that limited their freedom to plan and direct their projects. Also consultants who provided expert advice but who had no accountability to their clients, often confused the organizing committees and weakened their capacity to use their own common sense.

The most significant support of governments to the formation of the Evangeline co-operatives was the funding of the development organizations and also the provision of both project development and operational funding to the co-operatives themselves. The Co-operative Council received funding from the federal Department of the Secretary of State, and the Baie Acadienne Industrial Commission from the provincial Department of Industry. The potato chip co-operative obtained funding to study the project's feasibility, and the cable co-operative to hire project staff to conduct surveys and to recruit members for the co-operative. In addition to project development assistance, three of the four co-operatives received a major portion of the capital they required from government sources. The potato chip co-operative raised approximately half of its financing within the Evangeline region. Yet without the $500,000 received from government the potato-chip plant could not have been built. Similarly the training grant that Chez Nous obtained from the Department of Employment and Immigration was extremely significant, for it covered the cost of the labour to erect the building. With Les P'tits Acadiens, less than twenty-five per cent of the initial financing was raised locally. The majority of the financing came from government sources.

Government also provided direct support to the formation of the co-operatives through the services of staff and resource persons who were also community members. In their role as a government employees with development responsibilities, they simply continued to work as they always had. Consequently this situation does not illustrate the effectiveness of government staff in community development but rather the importance of filling institutional leadership positions from the community.

Government funding was necessary for the formation of the potato chip co-operative and Les P'tits Acadiens, important for Chez Nous, and helpful for the cable co-operative. However, when it was provided in ways that directed local definitions of needs and solutions, it had detrimental effects. Funding that was tied to specific departmental or program objectives was not flexible enough to meet local needs. As an example, training grants from Employment and Immigration Canada were only available for the creation of full-time employment. No training funds were available for persons wishing to set up a part-time operation. As noted, for Les P'tits Acadiens the acceptance of a grant from Employment and Immigration meant that the co-operative could not consider the possibility of members working part-time out of their homes. They had no choice but to set up a full-time factory-type operation. Consequently, the effect of this grant was to remove control of the planning and decision-making from the initiating group. Rather than assisting the initiators to achieve their objectives, the requirements of the grant caused them to modify those objectives. The grant that Les P'tits Acadiens received from the P.E.I. Development Corporation for the purchase of equipment had a similar effect, since it required the purchase of new equipment. Essentially these grants limited the opportunity of the initiators to carry out a self-reliant planning process, which would have allowed them to examine alternatives and to select the best option. As the acceptance of this grant was the only way to obtain a year of guaranteed employment, the planning process of the co-operative was compromised.

In attempting to obtain funding from Canada Mortgage and Housing Corporation, Chez Nous faced a similar dilemma. Partial funding was available on the condition that the co-operative arrange to have the community care centre designed by an architect at considerable additional cost. As members of the planning committee had a clear understanding that they wished to proceed in as self-reliant a manner as possible, they did not allow the funding criteria to influence their objectives and they did not apply for the grant. This same clarity of purpose may be seen in Chez Nous' decision not to proceed with construction until there was sufficient funds to ensure that the monthly fees to residents of the proposed seniors' home were no more that $870. Members made this decision in the full knowledge that the co-operative might lose the Section 25 grant from Employment and Immigration for the costs of construction.

In a study of the impact of government programs upon co-operatives, Hammond Ketilson et al. (1992) also found that government funding based upon predetermined program criteria was detrimental to community economic development. Conditional funding, which redefined project objectives, weakened local commitment and had a negative impact upon project success. Hammond Ketilson suggested that instead of offering 'specific programs' to communities, a more useful role for government would be to respond to 'initiatives' from communities. The provision of external consultants and resource persons by government also can have a limiting effect when they are not accountable to the people they serve. Hammond Ketilson found that an emphasis on external consultants, who have no responsibility to a local constituency, can work against self-reliant development strategies. While the importance of government funding to the formation of these co-operatives is unquestionable, the impact of that funding upon project sustainability is less clear. It seemed that such assistance promoted self-reliance when initiators and community were determined to accomplish something and had made strenuous efforts of their own, in advance of receiving government funding. Government assistance may have promoted dependence when its availability motivated initiators to pursue something that they would not otherwise have attempted. One of the initiators of Les P'tits Acadiens reported that she probably would not have pursued her idea to start the co-operative if her husband (a government employee) had not said: 'The money's there.' Also the commitment of $1,000 made by each worker-member of Les P'tits Acadiens was relatively small in relation to the potential benefits of the training grant, which guaranteed each person a full year's employment.

Conversely with Chez Nous, the initiators began their local fund-raising efforts in advance of pursuing grants. They were determined to achieve their objective with or without external assistance. In these two co-operatives there seems to have been a connection between the extent of local commitment and the usefulness of external funding. Evidence of such a relationship is less clear with the P.E.I. Potato Chip Co-operative because, even though there was a high degree of local commitment, the co-operative failed. In that case, workers, the local financial institu-

tions, and the provincial government made substantial commitments. The costs of initiating the project were so high that even
with the greatest level of local commitment, the project could not
have proceeded without government help.

Co-operative Organizations

In addition to government agencies, established co-operatives
are an important type of external support organization. Until
recently, Co-op Atlantic (the second-tier wholesaler) did not have
a mandate or a strategy to support community-initiated co-operatives that were not retail organizations. In its informal agreements
to display Les P'tits Acadiens' clothes at its Moncton show or to
sell Olde Barrel potato chips under the Co-op label, Co-op Atlantic offered goodwill but not partnership. There was no recognition on the part of Co-op Atlantic that it shared responsibility for
the welfare of the community-initiated co-operatives. When Les
P'tits Acadiens' clothing was not displayed at Moncton, there was
no apology or attempt to make amends. When some complaints
about Olde Barrel chips were received, the product was simply
removed from the shelves and the contract with the potato chip
co-operative terminated. In what was aptly described by Tom
Webb of Co-op Atlantic as a 'charity model' of co-operation, it
seems that Co-op Atlantic was willing to be of service to
community-initiated co-operatives as long as there was little
inconvenience or expense to itself. There was no basis for mutuality. Community co-operatives had no right to a claim on Co-op
Atlantic's resources. By its actions, Co-op Atlantic showed that it
was not prepared to assist the community-initiated co-operatives
in any significant way to become successful.

Yet since access to markets was the critical factor for the
Evangeline worker co-operatives, a commitment of technical
and managerial and sales expertise on the part of Co-op
Atlantic might have made the difference between success and
failure. Such a commitment would have made it unnecessary
for the potato chip co-operative to incur the tremendous
expense of establishing its own sales distribution system. What
seems to have been missing was the recognition by Co-op Atlan-

tic of a role for itself in community-initiated co-operative development.

As of 1990, this began to change. At its 1990 annual meeting, Co-op Atlantic adopted the 'Proposal for Renewal' statement, which marked the first shift by established co-operatives toward support for community-initiated co-operative development. According to the managing editor of *The Atlantic Co-operator*, Brenda MacKinnon (Oct. 1992, 6), Co-op Atlantic now stands for 'integration of co-operatives, a bigger role for co-operatives in all sectors of the economy and co-operative development for social purposes.' In practical terms Co-op Atlantic's policy change has meant that it has taken an active role to promote the formation of local co-operative development councils throughout the Maritimes. Typically these councils include all types of co-operatives, including credit unions, producer co-operatives, worker co-operatives and housing co-operatives. Following the Evangeline Co-operative Council's lead, their role is to identify and to facilitate the potential for co-operative development in the area (Roy, Dec. 1992, 8). While other members of the Atlantic Council of Co-operatives (most notably the credit union centrals) have not yet agreed to participate in this development thrust, Co-op Atlantic has produced a manual for the co-op development councils and has hired an Initiatives for Renewal Co-ordinator to provide the councils with resource support. In addition staff members of established co-operatives have agreed to act as volunteer co-ordinators of the local co-operative development councils (Roy, Dec. 1992, 8). It is still premature to determine whether these initiatives by Co-op Atlantic will produce the intended impact upon community economic development.

CONCLUSION

In reviewing the proposed theory, each of the elements may be viewed as adding to the probability that community economic development (social, cultural, and economic) will occur. Although each of the three elements (community consciousness, empowering activities, supportive structures) add to the probability of this development, the proposed theory suggests that if any of the three elements is absent it is unlikely that community economic development will occur in any sustained manner. Community consciousness may be a requisite, but without empowering activities and supportive structures, community consciousness will be insufficient. Similarly, a community may have supportive structures, but without empowering activities and community consciousness, development that builds local leadership and community spirit is unlikely.

Moreover, these three elements, which have a particular form in the Evangeline context, may take on a different form in another context. For example, within Evangeline, community consciousness is tied to the cultural, linguistic, religious, familial, and historical commonalities of the people. However, within another community consciousness may occur for other reasons, such as a common concern for the survival of the community because of a declining economy or, for example, because of a common bond of association around such concerns as the environment, gender equality or 'at risk' youth or children. As these latter examples suggest, these bonds of association might not be bound by a geographic community but rather might be tied to a community of interest (Quarter 1992) that goes beyond a specific locale such as Evangeline. A labour union is an example of a community of common interest that can initiate projects for its members.

Therefore, it is proposed that this theory is not only applicable to co-operative formation within a geographically defined community but may be applicable to community economic development more generally, and including enterprises other than co-operatives and for communities of common interest as well. Within those contexts, as in Evangeline, there will be a need for empowering activities and supportive structures. However, as with community consciousness, these elements may be manifested by means other than those at Evangeline.

5

From Theory to Practice

The theory presented in chapter 4 differs from many others on co-operative formation in so far as it focuses on the actual process of developing co-operatives, not in isolation but rather in the context of a community with a tradition for such initiatives. The theory is based on a combination of structural and intentional factors, and in that respect differs from the emphasis in the literature on structural conditions that are believed to determine development. While there is some disagreement on specifics, much of the literature stresses the importance of inadequacies or conflicts in the economic system as major determinants of co-operative formation. Some factors that these studies suggest as causative of co-operative formation are industrial depression and unemployment (Shirom 1972); the development of monopoly capitalism, which displaced self-employed craftpersons for wage labour, decreased job security, and heightened the distance between employees and employers (Aldrich and Stern 1983); and development of a means to resist employers' efforts to exclude unions and cut wages (Grossman 1943).

Most specific of all was Sacouman's (1976) explanation of the formation of the Antigonish Movement co-operatives in the Atlantic region of Canada. He rejected explanations based on generalized social distress or charismatic leadership, and instead argued that these co-operative movements were 'collective responses to specific forms of capitalist underdevelopment' (1990, 38). For Sacouman it was the conflict generated by capitalist working-class relations that provided 'the principal social basis for the incidence of the Antigonish Movement co-operatives and credit unions' (1976, 234).

In addition to economic forces, the literature suggests a number of other factors that affected the formation of the co-operatives. Shirom (1972) points out that the dominant business environment has been actively hostile to collectively owned businesses. Taking a similar tack, Aldrich and Stern (1983) suggest that collective entrepreneurship is at a disadvantage in relation to individual entrepreneurship because the societal context favours material incentives over solidary and purposive ones. They indicate the necessity for the mobilization of political and economic resources as a means to counteract the North American cultural bias toward individualism. The kind of mobilization of resources required to establish industrial co-operatives has not taken place because political movements supportive of collective entrepreneurship strategies have been too weak and labour unions too ambivalent.

Fairbairn (1990) cites two additional causes of co-operative formation: shared social interests and minority culture. Historically, co-operatives have been established by a specific interest group (usually farmers, fishers, or other groups of working people), which have a common social outlook 'based on collective aspirations or exclusion from economic structures' (63). When co-operatives have been formed by people with more varied social interests (as in Evangeline, for example), this has been on the principle of 'minority culture and solidarity' (74).

The most comprehensive theoretical explanation for the formation of co-operatives is advanced by Jösch (1983). Drawing a comparison between the German co-operatives of the 1850s and newer food co-operatives, Jösch suggests that six conditions are needed for consumers to organize co-operatives: threats to economic position; an understanding that the cause of these threats is societal rather than individual; aspirations that include the social and cultural, as well as economic; knowledge of ideas and models that provide hope; intensive interaction with other community members and the opportunity to participate and be involved; and support systems that provide advice and information.

With the exception of Jösch's work, the literature on the establishment of co-operatives does not address the actual process of co-operative formation. It is, however, helpful in identifying a number of factors that appear to have contributed to the formation of co-operatives in specific historical situations. In terms of providing definitive explanations of co-operative formation, the literature is inadequate. The theories based upon structural explanations demonstrate neither how structural conditions lead to action nor how macro conditions are linked to consciousness and activism. These structural explanations assume that human consciousness and action are largely determined by the push of economic forces. Such a view minimizes the importance of human motivation and intentionality that is not derivative of the material relations of production. While structural explanations might have some validity, they are unable to account for the process of co-operative formation in a specific situation. A study by Conte and Jones (1985) concurs with this view. They tested a number of theories, including those of Shirom (1972), Grossman (1943), and Aldrich and Stern (1983), which claimed to explain the formation of U.S. producer co-operatives. Without exception, they found that all the theories had poor explanatory power. They concluded that it is unlikely that causative relations between 'the formation rate' of co-operatives and 'specific objective phenomena' can be established (378).

In a similar vein, Fairbairn (1990) suggests a greater role for human intentionality. For him co-operatives are also a political means for changing societal structures and achieving participation for the excluded. They are not only reactive responses to the material forces of the economy, but proactive initiatives 'to achieve participation in society as a whole' (132). In fact, the major study of the Mondragon co-operative system in the Basque region of Spain by Whyte and Whyte (1988), although not dismissing structural factors, also tends to come down on the important role of human intentionality as an explanation for development.

Our theoretical explanation for community economic development in Evangeline (chapter 4) also combines the intentional and the structural. Bearing that in mind, one is better able to consider the implications for practice – but with one caveat that is stated in advance. Although the theory advanced in this study has implications for practice, it would be inappropriate to attempt to reduce those implications to an oversimplified formula of what to do and not to do. There are some general understandings that have been derived from the Evangeline experience that form the basis for the practice of community economic development, not only in Evangeline but also in other communities. However, these understandings cannot be reduced to a mechanistic check-list that practitioners can follow in a lock-step manner. The model proposed in this manuscript provides some insight as to the factors that must be in place for successful community economic development, and the case studies highlight the steps that may be taken by practitioners operating within a context that contains the elements needed for success. However, the intentional aspect of community economic development always involves the need to work with the unique needs of the context and the participants. As such the recipe will always vary.

IMPLICATIONS FOR COMMUNITY ECONOMIC DEVELOPMENT

Let us begin with community consciousness and its two components of a movement perspective and community attachments. While these characteristics grew out of Evangeline's historical and cultural context, and therefore are arguably structural factors, they were not automatically locked in by the culture. Rather the evidence, both historical as well as from the four case studies, suggests that community consciousness was preserved by members of the community through deliberate efforts and sustained struggles against hostile external influences. Arguably these hostile external influences, as well as the other structural conditions that contributed to community consciousness (for example, economic deprivation, a common culture, a common minority language, and a common religion), affected the ability of residents of the community to initiate projects that in turn preserved community consciousness. In other words, community consciousness (as a structural factor) increased the probability that members of Evangeline would initiate community development projects, but without the energetic response of the residents community consciousness would have lost its vibrancy and eventually have become a spent force.

But what happens when a community lacks community consciousness, or at least in sufficient degree to initiate community development projects? Can community leaders or other animators foster its development? The answer to that question is not clear from the study of Evangeline because it is a community in which community consciousness, and its components of community attachments and a movement perspective, are already strong. The evidence from Evangeline that community consciousness must be nurtured by the actions of the residents in order to be sustained, while suggestive, does not necessarily mean that it can be fostered in a community that lacks such traditions. Although the essential lesson from Evangeline is one of hope and of the strength of human intentionality, as noted, human intentionality operates within structures or traditions. Where such traditions are non-existent, it would be more difficult to construct a strong sense of community consciousness from scratch.

However, this latter statement should not be interpreted to mean that community economic development can occur only in a tightly knit community such as Evangeline. Although community consciousness in Evangeline was tied to the struggle for linguistic and cultural survival (as is the case, for example, in northeastern New Brunswick, northern Ontario, native communities, and other pockets of minority culture), other communities discover their own sources of solidarity. In rural Saskatchewan, where the crisis in agriculture threatens many communities, economic need may be a source of community consciousness. In the Newfoundland outports and other Atlantic villages, the decline of the fisheries is forcing community consciousness. In parts of the country where the economic problems are chronic (for example, Cape Breton), again one finds community consciousness developing around common economic crises.

In addition to cultural, linguistic, and economic factors, community consciousness may also result from regional loyalties, or a sense of 'we-ness,' derived from both the positive attachments that people have to their geographic location as well as past efforts to find solutions to common problems. The current shift toward globalization, both of the marketplace and other political institutions, is threatening to the local ties that have been fostered over generations. Within this context communities are coalescing around a desire to retain some control over the institutions that govern them (Laxer 1993). The rejection of amendments to the Canadian constitution and the present support for populist politics may indicate not only citizens' resistance to top-down approaches to change enacted by elites but also their aspirations to participate. This desire of people to be involved in decisions that affect their lives signals a new importance for strategies of regional and community self-reliance.

All of the examples to this point pertain to geographic communities. However, within the modern world the most common type of community arrangement is through aspatial networks in which groups of people coalesce because they share a common interest or need. Generally such arrangements are very specific (as contrasted to geographic communities that tend to be more comprehensive), involve many features of people's lives, and are situated in urban locales (Quarter 1992). The oldest form of aspatial community was a mutual benefit society in which people with a common need (for example, burial services, insurance) formed an organization to serve its members. Religious congregations, ethnocultural societies, social clubs, trade unions, and professional and business associations are other examples of mutual associations. Although such societies involve a type of community consciousness, it is doubtful whether they can ever achieve the degree of local solidarity found in a community such as Evangeline. Nevertheless, in some respects they are a more important phenomenon than geographic communities because they have the potential for linking community economic development to the broader movements for social justice and environmental sustainability. A comprehensive community economic development perspective with transformative potential would recognize the interdependence of the local community with all other earth communities and the natural world. According to Friedmann (1992) an adequate vision of development 'is not limited to local actions warding off immediate threats to life and livelihood. It also pursues the transcendent goals of an inclusive democracy, appropriate economic growth, gender equality and sustainability' (164). From this it follows that community economic development must be part of a broader vision of social change.

Although Evangeline was in many respects an insular community, community consciousness was not simply based upon local needs but was also part of a much broader social movement to preserve the Acadian culture. Evangeline also located itself within the broader co-operative movement, both in Canada and internationally, and participated in broader movements for social justice through international work in assisting the development of co-operatives in Haiti. Although it would have been possible to have a strong sense of community consciousness without this broader sense of movement, the movements within which Evangeline participated enriched the consciousness of the local community.

Based upon this study of Evangeline, it would be difficult to argue that community consciousness can be fostered in some mechanical way. Nevertheless, Evangeline also suggests that community consciousness can be stimulated with the assistance of animators who assist residents to identify their common needs and agendas for common action. However, this suggestion must be put in perspective because there is a limit to which an animation process can alter the traditions of a community, particularly when the bonds of association are superficial or not based upon harmonious relations.

There is another point that should be emphasized. Even though community consciousness may be viewed as a prerequisite of community economic development, it is not sufficient without empowering activities and supportive structures. There are many tightly knit communities such as Evangeline that lack the thrust to local development.

EMPOWERING ACTIVITIES

Empowering activities (involvement and self-reliance) reflected the intentional or activist characteristics of Evangeline residents in defining their future. Yet even these activities operated within a structural context that enhanced the probability of their initiation. There was a tradition for such activities, support for them from both key institutions and residents of the community, and an expectation on the part of their initiators that they would be supported. Even though these activities were intentional, they operated within a context that made the probability of these actions more likely.

The utilization of involvement strategies, which were deliberately and carefully organized, indicate that initiators recognized that even with the Evangeline region's exceptional community consciousness, participation would not happen without effort. Often their involvement activities linked self-interest and community interest so that the moral imperative to participate was strengthened by that of personal interests. One implication of the Evangeline experience is that if community support is considered important, it must be actively sought. Initiators of community economic development must develop a planned strategy to elicit participation. In practical terms this means that significant resources must be directed to this central function to ensure that it is not neglected. It also means that since people are motivated by different stimuli, a wide variety of activities will be required to obtain broad community participation.

A second aspect of the Evangeline region's involvement strategies was the emphasis placed upon community-wide participation. Information was widely shared, decisions were taken at open public meetings, and an emphasis was placed upon outreach. The implication from this strategy is that projects must be open to public input. Community members must be informed and must feel that there is a place for them. Even when a group has been assigned a specific task, its recommendations should be open to public scrutiny and approval. A variety of involvement strategies used in Evangeline could be adopted more generally: a community newsletter; ensuring that major decisions about community projects are taken by a majority vote in open public meetings; and using personal contact to solicit community members' participation.

Self-reliant strategies, the second component of empowerment, also were essential to the development process. One such strategy was the Evangeline region's provision of its own essential services, primarily through its co-operative organizations. This benefited the community by creating employment and preventing income from leaking out of the community. At the same time it may have disadvantaged individuals by depriving them of the greater choice and the marginally lower prices found in larger centres. The implication of this import substitution strategy for community economic development is not only the maintenance of employment, but the capture of management functions by the community as well. This strategy assists communities to enhance their leadership infrastructure, without which development is not likely to occur. As has already been suggested, this strategy is unlikely to be successful without intensive efforts to construct a community consciousness.

A second self-reliant strategy was the utilization of local human and financial resources to the greatest extent possible. In the Evangeline region, when co-operatives have been formed to provide necessary community services with the major inputs from local human and financial resources, the results have invariably been successful. Unfortunately, export-oriented co-operatives have experienced much less success. An over-dependence upon external financial resources, and the absence of partnership arrangements to supply required technical skills and access to secure capital have been the main reasons for this lack of success.

There are several implications for community economic development from this finding. It appears that there is likely to be greater community support for services that are seen to benefit most members of the community. There is also likely to be greater commitment to the project when local people and local financing have played the lead role. The implications of the failure of the Evangeline region's export-oriented co-operatives for community economic development are more complex. With respect to financial resources, it seems that in order to be successful a project must either have the necessary expertise within its membership or have the opportunity to access the expertise as needed. With respect to external financial resources, it seems that there must be evidence of solid local commitment for the project as well as a business plan that demonstrates the likelihood of success before external resources are made available. Moreover, it seems that external partnerships are necessary for export-oriented projects. Unless such community-based projects are connected to a collaborative structure that has the capacity to provide consulting expertise and emergency financing if required, they are not likely to survive. Communities must either participate in such structures or be content with projects that focus upon meeting community needs.

A third self-reliant strategy was the mutual support that took place across the region. People from the various small communities that make up the Evangeline region worked together to form the co-operatives. Community organizations, government and non-government agencies, and private entrepreneurs all collaborated. Unlike Evangeline, however, most communities are not likely to support community economic development in such a wholehearted way. There will be private entrepreneurs and others who will view it as a threat, and some segments of the community might not be willing to support organizations that do not directly relate to their interests. Therefore, it appears that empowering activities are likely to be most effective when they operate within the context of a high level of community consciousness. In communities that lack the consciousness of Evangeline, it is important for the initiators of projects to attempt to bring the community together around the common goal of self-reliance for community benefit. Doing so means taking the high ground, in circumstances where there are differences within the community on a particular project, and attempting to build as much solidarity as possible.

One way in which communities create this solidarity is through initiating the types of projects described in this study, and particularly if these projects are successful and provide tangible benefits for a broad spectrum of community residents. Chez Nous was probably the best example among the four cases of a project that drew the community together, and thereby strengthened community consciousness.

IMPLICATIONS FOR SUPPORTIVE STRUCTURES

Community development organizations were the essential support structures for community economic development in the Evangeline region. They both responded to the initiatives of community members and acted proactively to stimulate community participation. They were effective in encouraging the formation of co-operatives because they mobilized resources specifically for this purpose. The implication of this finding for community economic development is that a local co-operative council or community development corporation can be an effective way to focus the energies of a community (or cluster of communities) upon a process of self-development. It must be clear that these organizations are not ends in themselves. While they may be multifunctional, their core function must be that of promoting community participation and interdependence. They exist to support community self-reliance, not to become a proxy for it. Finally, they must be perceived by the community to be democratic and accountable, and to belong to all sectors.

While the community development organizations were effective, they also had limitations, such as the lack of adequate staffing and financial resources. Without core funding for full-time staff, it is difficult for these organizations to realize their potential. In Evangeline, for example, the lack of full-time staff as well as business expertise made it difficult for development organizations such as the Co-operative Council to sustain co-operatives after the formation period. Without this capacity, the Council watched helplessly while Les P'tits Acadiens and the P.E.I. Potato Chip Co-operative floundered and went down. The implication of this experience is that local co-operative councils must have broader powers and the business expertise that is required. That type of arrangement is one factor that accounts for the success of the Mondragon co-operatives in the Basque region of Spain (Whyte and Whyte 1988).

A major limitation of the Evangeline Co-operative Council was its lack of a collaborative relationship with a body that might have been able to provide the resources it lacked. The implication arising from this situation is that local co-operative councils need to join together to create a regional or provincial support organization to which they would belong. Governments and second-level co-operatives provided important and, in some situations, essential support to community economic development in the Evangeline region. However, since the way in which support was provided was often inappropriate, the Evangeline experience suggests that governments' relationships to communities must undergo radical change. Government services were perceived to be helpful to community economic development when staff or other human-resource expertise was provided in an accountable manner. In such situations the capacity of community groups was strengthened. When, on the other hand, community groups were treated as recipients rather than as responsible participants, government services were seen to have a harmful effect.

The implications of this finding is that governments must either learn how to decentralize control so that authority over staff and services is shared with the community or they must get out of direct involvement in community economic development. The first suggestion envisions a kind of joint accountability of staff to both government and community, as in the Baie Acadienne Industrial Commission. Alternatively it might involve a type of secondment, where government staff would be responsible to the community's development organization. The second suggestion envisions that government resources would be transferred to local and regional or provincial community development organizations. With core funding for staff and human-resource expertise, these bodies would then provide themselves with the services they require.

Financial support from governments was perceived to be helpful when it assisted community groups to pursue objectives to which they had already demonstrated a commitment. Such support was found to be damaging and dependency-creating when it moulded local objectives to suit the governments' predetermined program criteria. There are two implications that flow from this experience. First, both evidence of local commitment and potential business viability should be taken into account in the decision to make available financial assistance. This evaluative information could be prepared for government by a provincial-level community development organization as an interested but impartial third party. Second, government financial resources must respond to community initiatives, not direct them. Programs must be flexible enough so that they can recognize the uniqueness of a particular community situation. If they are to make this accommodation, the funding should be transferred to the proposed regional or provincial community development organizations in the form of block grants.

Radical change is also required in the role of second-level co-operatives if community economic development is to move forward. Co-op Atlantic's lack of both a mandate and a strategy to support community economic development was demonstrated by its inability to respond in a useful way to the needs of the Evangeline region's worker co-operatives. As a consequence both of these co-operatives failed. One implication of this experience is that second-level co-operatives must expand their mandate to include co-operative development at the community level. Second-level co-operatives must also develop strategies to make necessary resources available to local co-operatives based on arrangements that embody the principles of mutuality and co-operation between co-operatives.

While the Atlantic region co-operatives have not yet agreed to co-ordinated efforts to support community economic development, Co-op Atlantic's provision of consulting services to the P.E.I. Potato Chip Co-operative after it went into receivership demonstrated a new commitment to community economic development. Since the potato chip co-operative failed in spite of these services, one possible implication is that such a strategy is insufficient and perhaps more comprehensive co-operative development strategies are necessary. Instead of Co-op Atlantic's staff providing consulting services on an overload basis, a bolder approach may be required. One possibility that has already been suggested is the establishment of regional or provincial co-operative or community development organizations. These new structures funded by both governments and co-operative organizations, and integrally connected with community-based co-operatives, would have the capacity to offer the broad range of services that community economic development requires.

GENERALIZING

The model outlined in this study, and the implications that flow from it, are based upon a region that possesses many unique features. These are a minority Acadian community, relative homogeneity across race, class, and religion, close interpersonal and organizational ties, and a successful co-operative tradition. Consequently further study of community economic development in dissimilar communities is needed to confirm the centrality of the elements that make up the suggested theoretical framework. In particular, it is important to determine whether such a model could be utilized in communities that lack the homogeneity of Evangeline, and even more so in aspatial communities in which people come together out of a common interest. Based on the current study, it would be presumptuous to say that the model could be generalized, that is, the set of practices developed in Evangeline could be used universally. On the other hand, it would be presumptuous to say that because Evangeline has its own unique qualities that the model cannot be utilized elsewhere.

Although Evangeline is a unique community the problems with which it is coping are not unique. Like other communities throughout the hinterlands of Canada it is coping with an international crisis in primary industries and an international trend toward the globalization that has encouraged businesses throughout the world to shift their production to areas of low per-unit costs. It is from this context that the community economic development movement has emerged. By analysing community economic development in Evangeline, and setting forth a framework of the components that are associated with development within this region, one may have at least the potential to see whether the framework is generalizable and whether it is a useful tool for informing practice.

Assuming that this framework, or a modified version of it, proves useful, it could then serve as an analytic tool to determine whether a particular community has the resources to move ahead with a community development strategy, and if there are deficiencies, what these are and how they might be remedied. For example, communities with community consciousness might lack supportive institutions that are basic for a successful community economic development. Before embarking upon particular projects, the com-munity might attempt to put these supports in place.

In other words, the framework that is presented in this study could serve as an analytic tool and heuristic device for community developers. Moreover, in attempting to apply the framework there will be new insights that will lead to modifications. To a degree this process already occurs. However, this framework may serve to formalize that process and move it from intuition to science. That is not to say that community development practices, are very much an art, can be reduced to mechanical formulae that eliminate intuition and spontaneity. However, it seems useful to attempt to formalize the understandings of successful practice so that others may utilize it. That is, the insights from Evangeline may prove useful in other communities.

CONCLUSION

This chapter has included a discussion of the implications of the Evangeline experience for community development practice. In Evangeline, community consciousness, one of the essential conditions for community economic development, was created and maintained through deliberate efforts and an ongoing educational process. While this may be more difficult to achieve in communities that lack Evangeline's traditions, this study suggests that the development of community consciousness is not only necessary but also possible in other communities.

The study also suggests that participation and self-reliance are the key activities through which community consciousness is maintained and through which community economic development projects are implemented. Even in Evangeline, participation does not occur automatically. To achieve it, a planned strategy is required and significant human and financial resources must be allocated. It is likely that such an approach will yield similar results in any community.

The Evangeline experience also suggests that self-reliant strategies are utilized to develop local capacity and to increase the likelihood of a co-operative's success. Similar strategies are likely to be important for community economic development elsewhere.

This study also highlights the significance of support organizations for successful community economic development. It found that community-controlled multifunctional organizations that both mobilize the community and provide consulting and financial services are an effective means to initiate and maintain development efforts. Such organizations require government funding of their core operations during the start-up period and until such time as they can become self-sustaining. They also require access to seed money for applied research leading to project initiation and evaluation.

Community economic development has the potential to revitalize rural and urban communities threatened by decay. However, for that to occur governments must put in place funding frameworks that communities can access to establish development organizations as well as to initiate projects. Further, since communities may want to produce goods and services, not only for their own needs but for sale in national and international markets, they will require specialized consulting services and greater access to capital than is available either through their own development organizations or from conventional sources. Consequently, regional or provincial support organizations are absolutely necessary to supply the consulting expertise and access to project financing. The Canadian co-operative movement and its member organizations are well placed to establish provincial-level community development organizations with the capacity to offer these services to communities. Alternatively, the established co-operatives could enter into partnerships with churches, unions, and other social organizations to launch support organizations.

To conclude, it is our hope that the study accomplishes three purposes: 1) that it increases understanding of the factors that contribute to community economic development and the way they operate to support or limit development; 2) that it stimulates experimentation and reflective action that benefits the practice of community economic development; 3) that it excites the imagination with the possibility that a democratically accountable economy that makes human and social needs a priority is not just an idea existing at the margins, but one that has transformative potential for the mainstream. Chomsky (1988) proposed that 'the task for a modern industrial society is to achieve what is now technically realizable, namely a society which is really based on free voluntary participation of people who produce and create, live their lives freely within institutions they control, and with limited hierarchical structures, possibly none at all.' Chomsky is setting out a idealistic agenda that some might even consider to be utopian. Although Evangeline has its limitations that fall short of Chomsky's ideal, to a considerable extent it operates in a manner that Chomsky is suggesting. For that reason, it seems important to attempt to learn from Evangeline's accomplishments.

Methodology

This study utilized a qualitative approach to investigate the phenomenon of co-operative formation. Data were obtained primarily from interviews and written records. Data analysis followed the procedures for decontextualizing and re-contextualizing in descriptive/interpretive analysis (Tesch 1990).

This study investigated the formation and development of four co-operatives in the Evangeline region of P.E.I. from the point of view of those who were most involved (initiators and members of organizing committees). Close attention was given to the details of the stories of these persons in order to gain an understanding of their actions, thoughts, and feelings, as well as their knowledge and understanding of external events and phenomena. Since the emphasis was on discovery, initiators and members of the co-operatives' organizing committees were asked to describe the process of co-operative formation and to suggest those factors that contributed to or limited this process. Their experience, perceptions, and knowledge of how these factors influenced co-operative formation were explored in depth.

RESEARCH PROCEDURES

Site Selection

The site was selected because it appeared to represent a successful example of the extension of democracy into the economy through community ownership and control of institutions and enterprises. It appeared to represent an alternate kind of development whose starting point was centred on people in relation to the community, and to recognize that social and cultural values are inseparable from economic values. This notion of alternate development has been captured by Friedmann (1992) as follows: 'Alternate development recognizes the interdependencies which exist between the rationality of economic reasoning and the moral relations that tie people's fates to each other at the intimate scale of kinship, friendship and neighbourly community.'

The first author visited Evangeline in February 1991. With the help of Amand Arsenault, manager of the Regional Services Centre, he was able to meet a number of Evangeline region co-operators during the visit. The positive tone of these meetings and the willingness of the people to participate in the research resulted in the decision to select the Evangeline region as the site.

Selection of Participants

Qualitative research uses criterion-based selection techniques rather than probabilistic sampling techniques since the intent is to generalize to theory rather than to populations (Moon et al. 1990). In this study the criterion for selection was the extent to which participants were able to further the study objectives. The study examined four of the co-operatives that have been formed since the inception of the Evangeline Co-operative Council in 1977. To obtain the greatest possible diversity among the cases, both service co-operatives with a community membership base and worker/production co-operatives, with membership limited to workers, were selected. The two service co-operatives studied were Chez Nous, a community-care facility for seniors, and the Community Communications Co-operative, which provided French-language cable television service. The two worker co-operatives were Les P'tits Acadiens, an enterprise that manufactured children's clothing, and the P.E.I. Potato Chip Co-operative, which processed local potatoes. Les P'tits Acadiens was chosen specifically because it had not been able to maintain itself successfully.

Since the process of co-operative formation and development
was the unit of analysis for this study, the participants selected for
interviewing were those persons most involved in starting the co-
operatives. The manager of the Co-operative Council provided
the names of the key initiators. The names were checked with
other informants and with the interviewees themselves. An
attempt was made to interview as many of these persons as possible. In the case of Chez Nous, five of the six people involved with
the organizing committee were interviewed, as well as three
members of the larger planning committee. For the cable co-
operative, five of the eight persons involved with the organizing
committee were interviewed, as well as the co-operative's first
president. For Les P'tits Acadiens, three of the five persons
involved with the organizing committee were interviewed.
Finally, in the case of the potato chip co-operative, four of the
seven members of the organizing committee were interviewed, as
well as one person from the first board of directors. In total, seventeen initiators and members of organizing committees or
boards of directors were interviewed. Of the total, five were
involved in the formation of two different co-operatives. Also,
eight of those involved may be classified as institutional leaders,
since they held paid leadership positions in the community (for
example, director of government or non-governmental agency or
manager of a co-operative). The other nine persons may be
described as volunteers. Finally, eight of those interviewed were
females, and nine were males.

In order to identify these people and to make arrangements to
contact them, a letter was sent to the Evangeline Co-operative
Council to request assistance in organizing the research. The manager of the Co-operative Council provided lists of those who had
been involved in the formation of the four co-operatives and particularly those who had been most active. The manager of the
Regional Services Centre, who had been the first manager of the
Co-operative Council, verified this information. Participants were
asked to suggest people who might be able to provide additional
information. Potential participants were contacted by phone.
Before each interview, participants were given a letter describing

the research project and the conditions of participation and then requested to sign a consent form.

Interviews

The interviews with initiators and members of the co-operatives' organizing committees followed a semi-structured format and ranged from forty-five minutes to two hours in length. The interviews were planned to have two parts: first, a narrative mode to describe the formation and development of a particular co-operative; and second, the posing and answering of specific questions arising from the study's investigative framework, which required a more analytic mode of response. In practice, the interviews could not be so neatly divided. In telling the story of the co-operative's formation, participants often touched on the questions to be asked in the second part of the interview. Rather than asking these questions again later, the interviewer followed the participants' lead. If, at the end of the narrative account, participants had not dealt with questions from the investigative framework, these questions were raised directly. At the end of each interview participants were asked to reflect upon and to summarize the factors involved in the formation and development process of the co-operatives.

For the most part interviews were held in people's homes, although some were held in office settings. Participants were eager to talk about the formation of co-operatives, so little prompting was required.

Document Review

Documents were used primarily to supplement and to check data obtained from participant interviews. Documents were particularly useful to establish facts, such as amounts of money contributed or the dates of specific events. Of the documents available, *La Voix Acadienne*, an Acadian newspaper published bi-monthly, was the most useful. Found in the archives of the Acadian Museum at Miscouche, the news reports of this publication provided ongoing accounts of the formation and development of Evangeline region co-operatives. *The Atlantic Co-operator*, published monthly, also provided useful information. Although this source was less complete, and sometimes duplicated *La Voix Acadienne*, the fact that it was printed in English was an advantage in doing the research.

Utilization of a co-operative's own internal documents was more problematic. Not only were all documents written in the French language, but they were often unavailable. Chez Nous, still in the formation stage, did not have extensive records. All records of Les P'tits Acadiens had been either lost or destroyed. The P.E.I. Potato Chip Co-operative, perhaps because of its financial crisis, was unwilling to have its records examined. Consequently, it was only with the Community Communications Co-operative that internal documents were readily available to supplement data from other sources.

Participant Observation

With the exception of one meeting of the Chez Nous' planning committee, it was not possible to directly observe the co-operatives' formation and development process. However, there were ample opportunities to observe community processes more generally, when the first author lived in Wellington during the month of August 1991, as well as during the three-week period in April 1992 when the interviews were conducted. During these periods it was not only possible to speak with members of boards of directors and managers of many Evangeline region co-operatives, but also to gain an understanding of community life through informal means, such as boarding with a local family, attending social, cultural, and religious events, going lobster fishing, and being invited for dinner and musical soirées by local families. Field notes were maintained of these events.

DATA ANALYSIS

Since the purpose of this study was to identify the factors associated with co-operative formation and to explain how they operated, an analytic approach was required that would lead to a better understanding of this phenomenon. Tesch (1990, 65) applied the label 'interpretational' to the analysis of research such as this whose purpose is meaning-making. Interpretational analysis can be subdivided into two types: one is concerned with 'the generation of hypotheses' (theory-building) and the other with 'the identification of patterns or the discerning of meaning' (descriptive/interpretive). The type of analysis utilized for this study may be described as descriptive/interpretive. The actual accomplishment of the analysis required two theoretically distinct operations. The first was a 'detailed examination' of the information describing the formation of the co-operatives. The second had to do with 'determining its essential features,' which in this case meant interpreting how the information fit together to support or limit the formation process (Tesch 1990, 116). Although these two operations might be thought of as separate, in practice data interpretation took place not only after the organization of the data but also as insights occurred during the data examination phase. The segmenting of the data ('decontextualizing') resulted in categories (factors) that were applicable to the four co-operatives studied. Study of the themes (content) within each of these categories and comparison across the four co-operatives ('re-contextualizing') provided the basis for an understanding of the phenomenon of co-operative formation.

Validity and Reliability

What is being observed in qualitative research is 'people's constructions of reality' (Merriam 1988, 117). Consequently the internal validity of such a study depends upon the researcher's being able to show that 'the interpretations ... are credible to the constructors of the ... realities' (Lincoln and Guba 1985, 296). While the primary data for this study have been participant interviews, both document review and participation observation have been utilized to the extent possible within the limitations already outlined.

While reliability is essential to establish the certainty of causal relationships, it is not a goal of qualitative research (Merriam 1988). Instead, qualitative research emphasizes 'dependability' or 'consistency' (Lincoln and Guba 1985, 288). Merriam says that this means 'the results make sense' (1988, 172). Also, following a suggestion of Merriam's, an audit trail was left in the research through a description of data collection, category derivation, and researcher decision-making.

While the strength of the qualitative approach lies in providing depth of understanding, its weakness lies in the lack of generalizability to other situations. However, Lincoln and Guba (1985) suggest that a detailed description of the study's context may permit a certain type of generalizability, which they refer to as transferability.

References

Aldrich, H., and R.H. Stern, (1983). Resource mobilization and the creation of U.S. producer's co-operatives, 1835–1935. *Economic and Industrial Democracy*, 4: 371–401.

Argents pour la Coopérative des croustilles. (1986, April 16). *La Voix Acadienne*, p. 1.

Arsenault, A. (1991, 19 February, 15 and 25 August), Personal communications.

Arsenault, G. (1989). *The Island Acadians, 1720–1980*. Charlottetown: Ragweed Press.

Arsenault, J. (1991, 24 August). Personal communication.

Arsenault, L. (1991, 24 August). Personal communication.

Arsenault, R. (1985, 12 June). Des organismes acadiens montrent leur opposition à l'introduction de câblodistribution par un étranger. *La Voix Acadienne*, p. 3.

– (1985, 21 August). Le câble dans la région Evangéline. *La Voix Acadienne*, p. 9.

– (1985, 4 December). Formation d'une nouvelle coopérative. *La Voix Acadienne*, p. 2.

– (1985, 11 December). On étudie les possibilités de mettre sur pied un centre de soins communautaire pour personnes âgées. *La Voix Acadienne*, p. 3.

– (1985, 18 December). De retour d'une visite industrielle à Philadelphie. *La Voix Acadienne*, p. 11.

– (1986, 5 February). L'idée fait son chemin. *La Voix Acadienne*, p. 3.

– (1986a, 19 February). Demande pour un centre de soins communautaire. *La Voix Acadienne*, p. 13.

- (1986b, 19 February). On s'oppose au projet de câblodistribution. *La Voix Acadienne*, p. 12.
- (1986, 6 April). Plus de 115 personnes veulent travailler à la coopérative de croustilles. *La Voix Acadienne*, p. 2.
- (1986, 30 April). La coopérative de câblodistribution recherche des abonnés – membres. *La Voix Acadienne*, p. 3.
- (1986, 16 July). On accorde le contrat de construction. *La Voix Acadienne*, p. 15.
- (1986, 22 October). La câblodistribution: Un pas de plus vers la réalisation. *La Voix Acadienne*, p. 3.
- (1986, 19 November). Le câble arrivera à temps pour Noël. *La Voix Acadienne*, p. 3.
- (1986, 10 December). La production de croustilles encore retardée. *La Voix Acadienne*, p. 3.
- (1987, 21 January). La coopérative 'Les P'tits Acadiens' est formée. *La Voix Acadienne*, p. 3.
- (1987, 1 April). Les croustilles 'Olde Barrel' seront bientôt sur le marché. *La Voix Acadienne*, p. 11.
- (1987, 22 April). Les nouvelles croustilles se vendent très bien. *La Voix Acadienne*, p. 2.
- (1987, 29 April). Les vêtements de la Coopérative 'Les P'tits Acadiens' seront bientôt mis sur le marché. *La Voix Acadienne*, p. 2.
- (1987, 21 October). De nouveaux marchés pour les vêtements 'Les P'tits Acadiens.' *La Voix Acadienne*, p. 3.
- (1988, 27 January). La coop de croustilles lance deux nouvelles saveurs. *La Voix Acadienne*, p. 3.
- (1988, Winter). Evangeline, Prince Edward Island, the uncontested cooperative capital. *Worker Co-ops*, p. 7.
- (1988, 30 March). On vent se renseigner sur l'établissement d'un centre de soins communautaire. *La Voix Acadienne*, p. 3.
- (1989, 7 June). Une très bonne année pour la coopérative de communications communautaire. *La Voix Acadienne*, p. 3.
Blakely, E.J. (1992, February). Community economic development: Tomorrow's economy today. Paper presented at the International Forum on Community Economic Development, Toronto, Ontario, 13 and 14 February.
Broadhead, D., F. Lamontagne, and J. Pieke (1990). *The local development*

organization: A Canadian perspective. Local development paper no. 19. Ottawa: Economic Council of Canada.

Bryant, C. (1992, 14 February). Personal communication.

Cape Breton Assessment Team. (1991). *From dependence to enterprise.* Sydney, N.S.: Enterprise Cape Breton.

Chomsky, N. (1988). *Language and politics.* Montreal: Black Rose Books.

Conte, M.A., and D. Jones (1985). In search of a theory of formation for U.S. producer co-operatives: Tests of alternative hypotheses. *Proceedings of the 37th annual meeting of the Industrial Relations Research Association.* Dallas: Industrial Relations Research Association. 377–84.

– (1991). *On the entry of employee-owned firms: Theory and evidence from U.S. manufacturing industries, 1870–1960.* Working paper 91/5. New York: Dept. of Economics, Hamilton College.

Cormier, A. (1987, 10 June). La coopérative de communications communautaires intensifiera son recrutement. *La Voix Acadienne*, p. 3.

Cornforth, C., A. Thomas, J. Lewis, and R. Spear (1988). *Developing successful worker co-operatives.* London: Sage Publications.

Cossey, K. (1990). *Co-operative strategies for sustainable communities: Community-based development organizations.* Sackville: Dept. of Geography, Mount Allison University.

Craig, J. (1993). *The nature of co-operation.* Montreal: Black Rose Books.

Croteau, J. T. (1951). *Cradled in the waves.* Toronto: Ryerson Press.

Daly, H., and J. Cobb, Jr. (1989). *For the common good: Redirecting the economy toward community, the environment, and a sustainable future.* Boston: Beacon Press.

Economic Council of Canada (1990). *From the bottom up: The community economic development approach.* Ottawa: Canadian Government Publishing Centres.

Ekelund, F.A. (1987). The property of the common: Justifying co-operative activity. Occasional paper of the Centre for the Study of Co-operatives, 87–02, Saskatoon.

Fairbairn, B. (1990a). Co-operatives as politics: Membership, citizenship and democracy. In *Co-operative organizations and Canadian society*, ed. M.E. Fulton. Toronto: University of Toronto Press. 129–40.

– (1990b). Social bases of co-operation: Historical examples and contemporary questions. In *Co-operative organizations and Canadian society*, ed. M.E. Fulton. Toronto: University of Toronto Press. 63–76.

Fraser, S. (1992). New co-operative keeps Olde Barrel rolling. *Atlantic Co-operator*, 58: no. 6, 1–2.

Friedmann, J. (1992). *Empowerment: The politics of alternative development.* Cambridge: Blackwell Publishers.

Gallant, A. (1992, 26 August). Personal communication.

Gallant, C. (1982). *Le mouvement coopératif chez les Acadiens de la région Evangéline (1862–1982).* Summerside, P.E.I.: *La Voix Acadienne* and Williams and Crue.

– (1991, February). Evangeline co-ops keep wolf from door. *Maritime Co-operator.*

Gallant, P. (1991, 25 August). Personal communication.

Galtung, J. (1989). Towards a new economics: On the theory and practice of self-reliance. In *The living economy: A new economics in the making,* ed. P. Ekins. London: Routledge. 97–109.

Grossman, J. (1943). Co-operative foundries. *New York History,* 24: 196–210.

Hammond Ketilson, L., M. Fulton, B. Fairbairn, and J. Bold. (1992). *Climate for co-operative community development.* Saskatoon: Centre for the Study of Co-operatives, University of Saskatchewan.

Hirsch, E. (1986). The creation of political solidarity of social movement organization. *Sociological Quarterly,* 27: 373–87.

Hirschman, A. (1970). *Exit, voice and loyalty: Responses to decline in firms, organizations and states.* Cambridge, MA: Harvard University Press.

Jenkins, J. (1983). Resource mobilization theory and the study of social movements. *Annual Review of Sociology,* 9: 527–53.

Jordan, J. (1989). The multi-stakeholder approach to worker ownership. In *Partners in enterprise,* ed. J. Quarter and G. Melnyk. Montreal: Black Rose Books.

Jösch, J. (1983). Konsumgenossenschaften und Food Co-operatives: Eir vergleich der entstehungsbedingungen von verbraucherselbstorganisation. From an essay review by Kai Blomqvist (1985), *Journal of Consumer Policy,* 8: 81–7.

Laforest, J. (1988, 2 November). Coop Atlantic réduit ses achats de 'chips' de l'île par plus de 50 pour cent. *La Voix Acadienne,* p. 2.

– (1991, 13 February). La coopérative de travailleurs 'Les P'tits Acadiens' ferme ses portes. *La Voix Acadienne,* p. 3.

- (1992, 5 February). Alcide Bernard éclairait certains points. *La Voix Acadienne*, p. 3.
- (1992, 6 May). Les produits Olde Barrel disparâitront-ils de nos super-marchés? *La Voix Acadienne*, p. 1.
- (1992, 1 July). On saura en septembre si on construit ou si on remet à plus tard. *La Voix Acadienne*, p. 3.
- (1992, 16 September). La construction du Chez-Nous débutera à condition. *La Voix Acadienne*, p. 3.

Laidlaw, A. (1961). *The campus and the community: The global impact of the Antigonish Movement*. Montreal: Harvest House.

Lauvrière, E. (1924). *La tragédie d'un peuple: Histoire du peuple acadien de ses origines à nos jours*. Paris: Goulet.

Laxer, J. (1993). *False gods: How the globalization myth has impoverished Canada*. Toronto: Lester Publishing.

Lincoln, Y., and E. Guba. (1985). *Naturalistic inquiry*. Newbury Park, CA: Sage.

MacKinnon, B. (1992, October). Co-op Development: The gauntlet is thrown. *Atlantic Co-operator*, p. 6.

MacLeod, G. (1989). Worker co-ops and community economic development. In *Partners in Enterprise*, ed. J. Quarter and G. Melnyk. Montreal: Black Rose Books.

MacNeil, T. (1991, October). *The socio-economic development of communities: The roles of co-operatives and governments*. Paper presented at the Conference of Ministers Responsible for Co-operatives, Summerside, P.E.I.

MacPherson, I. (1979). *Each for all: A history of the co-operative movement in English Canada, 1900–1945*. Toronto: Macmillan.

Max-Neef, M. (1991). *Human scale development: Conception, application and further reflections*. London: Apex Press.

McAdam, D. (1982). *Political process and the development of black insurgency, 1930–1970*. Chicago: University of Chicago Press.

- (1986). Recruitment to high-risk activism: The case of freedom summer. *American Journal of Sociology*, 92: no. 1, 64–90.

McCarthy, J., and M.N. Zald. (1973). *The trend of social movements*. Morristown, NJ: General Learning.

McNeill, C. (1991, 22 and 28 August). Personal communications.

Melynk, G. (1985). *The search for community*. Montreal: Black Rose Books.

Merriam, S. (1988). *Case study research in education: A qualitative approach.* London: Jossey Bass.

Moon, S. M., D.R. Dillon, and D.H. Sprenkle. (1990). Family therapy and qualitative research. *Journal of Marriage and Family Therapy,* 16: no. 4, 357–73.

Murray, R. (1992a, February). *Europe and the new regionalism.* Paper presented at the International Forum on Community Economic Development, Toronto, Ontario, 13 and 14 February.

– (1992b, 13 February). Personal communication.

M1 Rural. (1985, 5 September). Television Cablesystems Inc. *Guardian.*

New Economy Development Group Inc. (1993). *Community economic development in Canada: A different way of doing things.* Ottawa: National Welfare Grants Program, Human Resources Dept., Canada.

Olson, M. (1965). *The logic of collective action.* NY: Schocken.

P.D.G. Consultants. (1991). *Stratégie de mise en valeur des communications.*

Père Noël apportera-t-il un centre de soins communautaire à la région Evangéline? (1991, 7 August). *La Voix Acadienne,* p. 3.

Perry, S. (1987). *Communities on the way.* Albany: State University of New York Press.

Quarter, J. (1992). *Canada's social economy. Co-operatives, non-profits and other community enterprises.* Toronto: James Lorimer.

Roy, J. (1992, December). Local councils need unprecedented support. *Atlantic Co-operator,* pp. 1, 8.

Sachs, W. (1991). Re-defining development. *Ideas,* Canadian Broadcasting Corporation, p. 2.

Sacouman, R.J. (1976). *Social origins of Antigonish co-operative associations in eastern Nova Scotia.* Ph.D. diss. University of Toronto.

– (1990). *Restructuring and resistance from Atlantic Canada.* Toronto: Garamond Press.

Shirom, A. (1972). The industrial relations system of industrial co-operatives in the United States, 1880–1935. *Labor History,* 533–51.

Staff. (1868, April). *The Examiner,* p. 2.

Swack, M. (1992, February). Community economic development: An alternative to traditional development. Paper presented at the International Forum on Community Economic Development, Toronto, Ontario.

Tesch, R. (1990). *Qualitative research: Analysis types and software tools.* London: Falmer Press.

Van Vliet, B. (1990, April). Wellington members flock to opening despite storm. *Atlantic Co-operator,* p. 23.

Webster, G. (1977). Co-operation, co-operatives and credit unions: Their place in Island history. In *Exploring Island History.* Ed. H. Baglole. Belfast, P.E.I.: Ragweed Press. 175–94.

Whyte, W., and K. Whyte (1988). *Making Mondragon.* Ithaca, NY: ILR Press.

Index

CPSIA information can be obtained at www.ICGtesting.com
Printed in the USA
LVOW11s0049150515

438559LV00016B/337/P